George Crabbe:
A Critical Study

John Lucas

GREENWICH EXCHANGE
LONDON

Greenwich Exchange, London

George Crabbe: A Critical Study
©John Lucas 2015

First published in Great Britain in 2015
All rights reserved

This book is sold subject to the conditions that it shall not,
by way of trade or otherwise, be lent, resold, hired out or
otherwise circulated without the publisher's prior consent
in any form of binding or cover other than that in which it is
published and without a similar condition including this
condition being imposed on the subsequent purchaser.

Printed and bound by **imprint**digital.net
Typesetting and layout by Jude Keen Ltd., London
Tel: 020 8355 4541

Cover design by December Publications, Belfast
Tel: 028 90286559
Cover Image ©Mary Evans Picture Library

Greenwich Exchange Website: www.greenex.co.uk

Cataloguing in Publication Data is available
from the British Library.

ISBN: 978-1-906075-93-4

For Andy Jack

Newspaper reader

Give him the darkest inch your shelf allows
Hide him in lonely garrets, if you will, –
But his hard, human pulse is throbbing still
With the pure strength that fearless truth endows.

Edwin Arlington Robinson, 'George Crabbe'.

Contents

Introduction

In the middle of the eighteenth century, England's east coast, while not as cut off from London as places in the far north of the country, was certainly remote enough to feel isolated. Inland, it's true, there were towns whose inhabitants, at least those with money and education, led lives they could think of as civilized. But Aldeburgh, or Aldborough as it was then spelt, the small fishing town where George Crabbe was born in 1754, had precious few claims to culture. Most of those who lived in or around it either survived by scratching an existence from the soil or, more riskily, they put out to a sea still rich in fish but often dangerous to the boats that went in search of its salt bounty. Simply to look at the litany of surnames common to littoral Suffolk is enough to show how dependent generations were on fishing: Codd was a familiar patronymic, as was Herring. (Although the number caught each year had declined from the 3 million averaged a century earlier, herrings were still a staple part of the diet along that coast.) And then there was Crabbe.

Not that Crabbe's own father was a fisherman. But for his employment as a collector of salt-duties with a salary of £20 a year he was certainly dependent on the sea. And though in 1762 he began to send his son to school at Bungay, on the Suffolk-Norfolk border and some way from the coast, and then for two years, from 1766 to 1768, to a 'country boarding school' at Stowmarket, George Crabbe grew up accustomed to, and deeply affected by, the bleak coast around Aldeburgh. He is the great poet of its moods, its 'sad splendour', its storms, its mud-banks, sullen, slow-moving streams, its bony wrecks, its flora and, to a lesser extent, fauna; and he is also the great psychologist and social observer of those who lived along its shores.

With Crabbe a new kind of English poem comes into existence, a kind we more often associate with prose fiction. In fact at some time in the 1790s he wrote at least three novels, although at the request of his wife he burnt them and never afterward spoke of them, as a result of which we know next to nothing about their contents or style. (The couple's two youngest sons both died in 1796 and it seems that Sarah Crabbe, née Elmy, a stern Methodist, associated their deaths with the 'sinful' act of writing fiction.)

If, as some have speculated, the novels were examples of the then fashionable taste for the 'Gothic' – all haunted castles, dark forests, and terrified girls – they are very different from the detailed, sometimes remorseless, accounts of the interaction between people and place which feature in the poems Crabbe began to write early in the new century. These poems make him a great realist of English provincial life; so it should come as no surprise that he was intensely admired by, among others, the novelists George Eliot, Elizabeth Gaskell and Thomas Hardy. Moreover, Crabbe's probings into the dark recesses of the mind drew Dickens to him (though the Inimitable disavowed the influence); and his handling of dialogue in verse is one of several reasons why Jane Austen, on hearing of his wife's death in 1814, wrote that she could imagine herself becoming the second Mrs Crabbe.

With the exception of Byron, who called Crabbe 'Nature's sternest painter, and her best', poets were for a long time less sympathetic. Wordsworth thought that nineteen out of twenty of Crabbe's poems were 'mere matter of fact; with which the muses have as much to do as they have with a collection of medical reports, or of Law cases.' Coleridge said more or less the same thing when he noted that 'In Crabbe there is an absolute defect of high imagination; he gives me little or no pleasure.' But, to reverse Marianne Moore's dictum about poems, what Crabbe gives us is imaginary toads in real gardens;

as a literalist of the imagination he has few if any equals. And although the following paragraphs set out a brief resumé of his life, it is Crabbe's poetry that fascinates me, as it has done since I first came across his work in an essay on Peter Grimes by E.M. Forster, which I read in 1959 in Forster's collection *Two Cheers for Democracy*, and which, after I had immersed myself in the poetry produced by what Forster rightly calls Crabbe's 'uncomfortable mind', led me to produce *A Selection from George Crabbe*, first published in 1967.

There have been further selections since then, including the Penguin *Selected Poems*, edited by Gavin Edwards (1991), and one by Jem Poster for Fyfield Books. There is also a *Selected Letters and Journals*, (OUP), edited by Thomas C. Faulkner (1985), some critical studies of various worth, and a full-dress biography by Neil Powell, which supplements and in some necessary ways corrects the still attractive *Life* by Crabbe's son. This first appeared as part of the posthumous 8-volume *Collected Poems* published in 1834, two years after Crabbe's death, and in shorter form has been available in modern editions put out by World's Classics and, subsequently, the Cresset Press. Interest in Crabbe has not abated. But he is perhaps best known as the author of 'Peter Grimes', because of Britten's opera, which, however fine its incidental music and some of the arias, is an intellectual and imaginative muddle.

This is a matter to which I shall inevitably return. But the first task is to set out, as briefly as possible, Crabbe's early years and his emergence as a poet.

1

Early years

I

After Crabbe's formal education ended in 1768 he spent three years apprenticed to an apothecary and farmer at Wickhambrook, then transferred the apprenticeship to a surgeon-apothecary at the handsome country town of Woodbridge, where he remained until 1774. Johnson's *Dictionary* defines 'apothecary' as 'a man who keeps medicines for sale'. Such medicines would have been largely prepared by the apothecary himself or his assistant, and were often, perhaps usually, concocted from wayside herbs, flowers and plants, dried and reduced to powdered form. It is easy to dismiss this as quackery, and no doubt many remedies were, if not worse than the illness they were meant to cure, at best placebos. In this sense, apothecaries' shops were the high-street chemists of their day, though there is no reason to doubt that those who ran them believed in the efficacy of at least some of their medicines, especially as they were derived from Herbals which had as much authority as, say, *Gray's Anatomy*, was to have for later generations of medical students.

It was an authority which long survived the eighteenth century. When in the late 1930s the eighteen-year-old Patrick Leigh Fermor set out to walk across Europe, he claimed the one book he took with him was *Culpeper's Herbal*, first published in 1622, which identified the medicinal value of just about every known plant and flower. According to Leigh Fermor, acting on the advice he found in Culpeper he was able to cure himself of whatever ailments he picked up on his travels.

Crabbe must have derived at least some of his seemingly inexhaustible knowledge of plant life from his apprentice days. In later years he would publish a number of papers on the flora of his native county, and though it was an age when interest in natural history became something of an obsession for many men, Crabbe's passion as well as his knowledge, ran deep. But he aspired to more. His aim was to become a surgeon. Why not? It paid better and was a profession rather than a trade. Though he probably knew that Smollett had been a ship's sawbones, he may not have been aware that Goldsmith claimed to have qualified as a surgeon at the University of Utrecht, any more than Keats, who also hoped to be a surgeon, knew of Crabbe's ambition, but for some poets – diagnosticians who peer into the dark recesses of the human heart – the medical profession holds a certain allure. In the twentieth century, William Carlos Williams, Miroslav Holub, and Dannie Abse, are three of many men who combined medicine with poetry in their long careers.

Crabbe's ambition to improve his social standing, which qualification as a surgeon would certainly have brought him, may have been given a particular push by his meeting in 1772 with the woman he was eventually to marry. Sarah Elmy, three years his senior, sometimes stayed with wealthy yeoman farmers in their house at Parham, near Woodbridge. In September of that year Crabbe published three poems, which seem to mark his first appearances in print. 'A Poetical Essay on Hope' and 'To Mira' (his classicising name in print for Sarah – an odd one given that the classical 'Myrrha' was changed into a turtle because of an incestuous love affair with her father), were published in Wheble's *Lady's Magazine*, while a rival journal, Robinson's *Lady's Magazine*, took 'Solitude'. These journals testify to the rapid expansion of literature aimed at women – a feature of eighteenth-century life. Ladies' journals were intended for the leisured class of married women who, forming to all intents and purposes a new phenomenon of the nuclear family – husband, wife, and children – and who, with servants to attend to all domestic chores, found time heavy on their hands. The contents of journals aimed specifically at them were meant to provide instruction as well as idle pleasure. Articles on etiquette alternated with ones on history and homiletics. Literature, whether in prose or verse, was intended to be of the improving kind.

The phenomenon of journal literature is part of the century's rapidly expanding print industry. There were newspapers, weekly and monthly magazines at both local and national level. Not only that. Book publishing was becoming a business. More or less every town had its bookshop and most shops doubled as publishers. And to fill the pages of the ephemera and provide the contents of books there was inevitably a growing army of scribblers. Grub Street runs through the eighteenth century and Crabbe would soon become one of its denizens.

He wanted to marry Sarah Elmy. But in 1772 he must have felt himself a long way from being acceptable to her family. In the years immediately following his meeting with her they seem to have come to an 'understanding'. But marriage for a young man with no money and few prospects was out of the question. For a while Crabbe worked as a labourer on the quay at Slaughdon, near Aldeburgh, then set up as an apothecary and surgeon without qualifications to the Aldeburgh poor. (Although in 1776 he attended medical lectures in London, that was as far as he got with his plans to become a medical man.) At the same time, according to Gavin Edwards, he 'starts to learn Latin seriously in order to read botanical books'. Then in 1780 he returned to London, this time in an attempt to become a published writer, one who would be able to earn a living by his pen.

In July of that year he published anonymously *The Candidate: A Poetical Epistle to the Authors of the Monthly Review*. It brought him no recognition, nor did it deserve to. *The Candidate* is poor work. Crabbe, it might seem, was about to become one more statistic in the Entry Column of 'failed writers', at whose head stood, or rather sat, poor Samuel Boyce, Hogarth's 'Distressed Poet', shown starving as he scribbles in his garret, on the bare floor of which lies an open copy of *The Grub Street Journal*. Hogarth's etching, which dates from 1737, gained new relevance when, in 1780, Herbert Croft published a novel, *Love and Madness*, the central section of which made the novel for a while compulsory reading because of its account of the death ten years earlier of the eighteen-year-old Thomas Chatterton, who had poisoned himself in his London garret. Almost at once, Chatterton became the image of the neglected poet-genius, the 'marvellous boy', in Wordsworth's phrase. No one reading *The Candidate* would think of applying those words to Crabbe.

II

Yet five years earlier he had written a far better poem. *Inebriety*, which was published anonymously by an Ipswich firm, sank without trace in 1775 and seems to have escaped the attention of virtually all critics and commentators since then. Here are the opening lines:

> The mighty spirit, and its power, which stains
> The bloodless cheek, and vivifies the brains,
> I sing. Say, ye, its fiery vot'ries true,
> The jovial curate, and the shrill-tongued shrew;
> Ye, in the floods of limpid poison nurst,
> Where bowl the second charms like bowl the first;

> Say how, and why, the sparkling ill is shed,
> The heart which hardens, and which rules the head.

As a piece of verse making in the manner created by Dryden and perfected by Pope, this has a good deal going for it. The couplet form, with its emphatic end-stopping, is saved from rhythmic dullness not only by the adroit use of verbs as rhyme words, which energises the syntax, but by the fact that Crabbe has already learnt how to make a sentence run over several lines so as to avoid a repeated stop-start judder. Besides, 'the jovial curate, and the shrill-tongued shrew', though they may seem stock types, are types not often found in poetry of the age. *Inebriety* in fact is a study, none too serious, of provincial life, or of its habits. Tongue-in-cheek, Crabbe gives his topers classical names – Flaminius, Curio – which, if it ridicules them, also suggests that their types are not unknown to history even if they're absent from most English poetry since Chaucer. Crabbe at one moment even seems to be on the side of his ale-house drinkers:

> Go, wiser thou! And in thy scale of taste
> Weigh gout and gravel against ale and rest;
> Call vulgar palates what thou judgest so,
> Say beer is heavy, windy, cold, and slow,
> Laugh at poor sots with insolent pretence,
> Yet cry, when tortured, where is Providence?

This is some way after Goldsmith in its attack on pomp, but it has an energy which is part of the management of the line – 'Weigh gout and gravel against ale and rest' – and is even funny.

But perhaps the best lines in the poem are those where Crabbe issues a mock-defence of beer.

> Lo, the poor toper whose untutored sense
> Sees bliss in ale and can with wine dispense;
> Whose head proud fancy never taught to steer
> Above the muddy ecstasies of beer.

Beer was indeed muddy, cloudy, even opaque, before a system of 'fining' was introduced, usually by casting iron filings over the surface of a barrel so as to draw down the impurities, and many breweries, small ones especially, were slow to introduce that process. Hence, the drinking salutation 'Mud in Your Eye'.

But what makes Crabbe's lines so felicitous is that they are a pastiche or parody of a passage in Pope's *Essay on Man* (1733-4).

> Lo, the poor Indian, whose untutored mind
> Sees God in clouds, or hears him in the wind;
> His soul proud science never taught to stray
> Far as the solar cloud, or milky way. (Epistle 1, lines 99-101)

So Crabbe had read Pope.

In fact, the young poet's debt to his great forebear is made clear in the opening lines of his poem. They are an intended mock-echo of the opening lines of Pope's 1729 *Dunciad*, itself a mock-echo of the opening of Virgil's *Aeneid* ('Arms and the Man I sing').

> Books and the Man I sing, the first who brings
> The Smithfield Muses to the Ear of Kings.
> Say great Patricians (since your selves inspire
> These wondrous works; so Jove and Fate require.)
> Say from what causes, in vain decry'd and curst,
> Still Dunce the second reigns like Dunce the first.

Crabbe's poem is in no sense a piece of juvenilia. Though it has its flaws – chiefly perhaps in an insecurity of tone, so that we're never quite sure how seriously he takes his subject – it is nevertheless a knowing, slyly allusive piece of work.

There is, though, so we may think, something a bit odd in Crabbe's taking as his model a poet who had died in 1744, ten years before he himself was born. What would we think of a poet born in 1975 who would choose to take as model, no matter how quizzically, *The Waste Land*? That he or she was behind the times? The question is worth putting because for the first third of the eighteenth century Pope had the kind of authority Eliot enjoyed roughly between 1920 and 1950. But, to quote Pope's great predecessor, Dryden, all human things are subject to decay, and by the middle years of the eighteenth century young poets were beginning to challenge and then discard Pope's influence. One of the most crucial moments comes with the publication in 1759 of Edward Young's essay 'Conjectures on Original Composition'. For Young to use the word 'original' in itself constitutes a challenge to Pope's authority – which after all was associated with his allegiance to a classical tradition of poetry, especially that of Augustan Rome, the city of Horace, Ovid, and Virgil.

Young pointed in a very different direction in order to locate true poetry's origins. He looked to the North – a largely mythic one, it's true, but nevertheless one whose very Gothic barbarousness was a challenge to Augustan values. Hence, Young's claim that there are two distinct kinds of poet. One is the 'scholar poet', who takes his ideas and models from Classical antiquity; the other, the 'divinely-inspired enthusiast', is the true genius. This kind of poet crosses 'all public roads into fresh untrodden ground'. The poet as genius, in other words, isn't beholden to the past. He looks ahead, chooses to be on his own, is the poet of solitude who will make his way unaided as he strikes out into the wild. From now on, in short, the true poet is likely to be an untutored genius, discounting the influence of earlier models, in particular those associated with a past Pope revered. He finds for himself where his true path lies.

I accept that in putting the matter this way I am sailing close to parody. The new poetry wasn't all hairy Gothicism, the melodious ravings of Ossianic primitives. Nevertheless, in the middle years of the eighteenth century there was one of the huge lurches in perception that went, with or anyway led to, the cultivation of an entirely new way of thinking about culture in general and, in particular, about poetry. From now on, raw, untutored 'genius' was widely held to be preferable to all the learning of schools. 'The tigers of wrath are wiser than the horses of instruction,' as Blake was famously to say in one of his Proverbs of Hell. And Blake, great poet and visionary, who was born a mere three years after Crabbe, was from a no more privileged background than was Crabbe. He too could be considered a self-made/self-taught man. It was Blake who said of Sir Joshua Reynolds, the law-giver of mainstream eighteenth-century art, that 'this man was hired to depress Genius'.

You might therefore think that Crabbe and Blake would have had far more in common than either had with a tradition which Blake despised. But in fact Crabbe never greatly wavered in his allegiance to it. From first to last he wrote in couplet form and he did so because that form could accommodate all he wanted to say. This could, of course, be put in negative terms. Wanting to identify himself with the Augustan tradition perfected by Pope, Crabbe turned his back on the actual life of those he was born and grew up among; he disguised himself so well as someone who belonged to the cultural orthodoxy that he inevitably became identified as inseparable from its values. Hence, we might think, John Clare's condemnation of Crabbe's depiction of the rural poor, included in a letter to his publisher John Taylor. 'What's he know about the distresses of the poor musing over a snug coal fire in his parsonage box.'

The answer is, far more than Clare realised, although he can be forgiven for his outburst, one to which I shall return. Here,

I want merely to note that the difference between Crabbe, on the one hand, and Blake and Clare, on the other, can't simply be put down to a matter of temperament, nor social circumstance. Though there are gradations between them, with Clare from the poorest of families, none was socially advantaged. Crabbe and Clare both came from provincial England, and they had to make their way as writers. (Blake's living was largely dependent on his work as illustrator for books which, as already noted, were an essential part of the new business enterprise of publishing.) What Crabbe's persistent use of the couplet *does* indicate, I think, is that poetic forms, like all artistic forms, while they may go in and out of fashion, can endlessly be adapted and re-fashioned so as to suit the moment. *The Waste Land* is a modern poem that seemed when it first appeared in 1922 to have killed off forms of English poetry associated with a discredited past. Ten years later Auden was writing in many of those forms in ways that couldn't possibly be thought of as out-moded.

It is, of course, true that more than one poet who aped Auden's use of metre, rhyme and stanza, produced poems that were dead on arrival. But that shouldn't surprise us, and it certainly shouldn't persuade us that formal poetry was itself moribund and that the future inevitably lay with *vers libre*, though that was what some critics and literary historians asserted, at all events those for whom Eliot had changed poetry as wholly as Einstein had changed our understanding of the physical universe. Besides, as any one who looks up poetry magazines of the 1930s will see, some poets who wrote in free verse, believing they had no alternative, produced verse as moribund as the direst work of formal poets. And by the same token, it can be said that for every true 'original' genius who appeared in the last thirty or so years of the eighteenth century – which probably means Robert Burns and, to a lesser extent, Robert Bloomfield – there were twenty or so whose glitter was that of paste diamond. (Beattie, Blair, Bridges ... and that's just the Bs, and by no means all of *them*.)

Wordsworth chose to write his early 'Descriptive Sketches' in couplets and the result is less than impressive:

> Gay lark of hope, thy silent song resume!
> Ye flattering eastern lights, once more the hills illume!
> Fresh gales and dews of life's delicious morn,
> And thou, lost fragrance of the heart, return!

Quite how you are supposed to become aware that a silent song has resumed, I wouldn't know. Presumably the poet means that the lark, who has fallen silent during the night, should, now that it's morning, awake and sing out once more. But the phrasing is as inept as the use of alexandrine – six stresses – in the line that follows, and the fustian of 'gales and dews' is as far from fresh as it's possible to be. So, it almost goes without saying, are those repeated exhortations to lark, lights, and lost fragrance, to be up and about. And there are getting on for seven hundred lines of this, as there are nearly four hundred of 'An Evening Walk', written in the same year and with similar lack of distinction.

Both 'Descriptive Sketches' and 'An Evening Walk' are dated to 1793, when Wordsworth was twenty-three years old. Both are identified in his Collected Poems as 'Poems Written in Youth'. This is intended as a disclaimer to ward off hostile critics from considering the poems as part of Wordsworth's mature *oeuvre*. Fair enough. But in that case we should recall that *Inebriety* is dated 1775, which means that when Crabbe wrote the poem he, too, was twenty-three. I am not about to claim that Crabbe is a greater poet than Wordsworth. He isn't. But he can handle couplets far better than Wordsworth ever could. Because where for Wordsworth couplets are merely a poetic fashion he is trying on – the couplet was still regularly used in the late eighteenth century for landscape poems, poetry of the picturesque – for Crabbe the couplet was a living, breathing expression. You could almost say it was a necessity. The great poet, Roy Fisher, once said that Birmingham, his native city, was what he thought with. The couplet was what Crabbe thought with. In *Inebriety* he tries various ways of making couplets work for him. One of the discoveries he makes is that he can get people to talk in a manner that feels flexible, plausible, and – most importantly – revealing. As when one of the topers, called Timon, says:

> Oh, place me, Jove, where none but women come,
> And thunders worse than thine afflict the room,
> Where one eternal nothing flutters round,
> And senseless titt'ring sense of mirth confound;
> Or lead me bound to garret, Babel-high,
> Where frantic poet rolls his crazy eye,
> Tiring the ear with oft-repeated chimes,
> And smiling at the never-ending rhymes:
> E'en here, or there, I'll be as blest as Jove,
> Give me tobacco, and the wine I love.

These ramblings of an old sot are, in their queasy way, an attempt at humour which neatly enough betrays his addled-headed silliness. I can put up with woman's noise, I can cope with the ravings of a Grub-Street poet, ho-ho, as long as I have some beer and baccy. It may not be great poetry but it does give an inkling of what Crabbe will do in later work, where dialogue is intrinsic to many of the poems. Reading 'Descriptive Sketches' you couldn't possibly guess that Wordsworth would become a great poet. But reading *Inebriety* you can see the beginnings of Crabbe's especial genius.

2

The 1780s

I

My argument about Crabbe's decision to use the couplet when most about him were abandoning it could, of course, be tilted to suggest that he did so because he was unaware of alternatives. He was on the side of the old because, growing up in a provincial backwater, he didn't know about new writing, new theories concerning poetry which were beginning to preoccupy London and the University cities.

But even if this was true of his earliest years – and I doubt that we will ever know what the young Crabbe read – this can't be the case once he moved to London in 1780, determined to succeed as a writer. You could, though, argue that the writing of *The Candidate: a Poetical Epistle to the Authors of the Monthly Review*, to give it its full title, in which he self-consciously sets out his writerly wares, suggests that the people he wants to impress are readers whose interests and indeed prejudices are conservative, perhaps with both small and large C. The poet with pen for hire announces himself as aware not merely of English poets – Dryden and Pope especially – but with a passable knowledge of Roman poetry, able to handle the heroic couplet, and keen to entertain 'polite' readers. And as *The Monthly Review* was one of the more successful journals of the age, and one which in its choice of contributors plainly championed conservative values, Crabbe's poem is tailored to meet its readers' approval.

This is what makes it so desperately dull. The poem is a kind of off-the-peg production. Look through anthologies of eighteenth-century poetry, including ones available to Crabbe himself, and you will find that *The Candidate* is virtually indistinguishable from many others being stitched together along Grub Street and offered for sale to a large and, perhaps, growing readership. Certainly, the compilers of these anthologies hoped, as did magazine editors, that the appetite for poetry was wide-spread enough to require constant supply; and the manufacturers of bookcases lived in equal hope.

Bookcases were, indeed, becoming fashionable items of middle-class households at precisely this time. Gentlemen had their libraries. (Mr Bennet of *Pride and Prejudice* is an example.) Others made do with cases, cases which housed specimens of rocks, of birds' eggs, of lepidoptera, of painted miniatures, of fossils, and of many other instances of collections made by men, and, less often women, who increasingly set themselves up as connoisseurs.

For this was the age of connoisseurship. Connoisseurship was a kind of learning. It was also evidence of good taste, and 'Taste' was very much an issue in the later years of the eighteenth century. Johnson, it is true, was sceptical of the connoisseur, as he was of most things French. In his Dictionary he allows the word in, but in italics. It isn't a true word. As for its meaning: 'Connoisseur: a judge; a critick; it is often used of a pretended critick.' But Johnson's scepticism was swept away by prevailing custom. Well before the end of the century the connoisseur was accepted as the correct term, for The Man of Taste as one who knew true from false. Hence, *The Library*.

II

Crabbe published this long and not very lively poem in 1781. But he did so under very changed circumstances from the previous year. Because early in 1781 he managed to introduce himself to the great Edmund Burke. That is to say, he called on Burke, gave him some of his verse to consider, and Burke was sufficiently impressed to act as patron to the young poet. In essence, this meant introducing Crabbe to influential friends, because Burke, Statesman, author of the *Philosophical Inquiry into the Origin of our Ideas of the Sublime and Beautiful* (1757), one of the great works of its age, was a close friend of Samuel Johnson. Before long, Crabbe was brought into the company not only of Johnson himself but introduced to others of Johnson's circle, including Sir Joshua Reynolds. He also met James Dodsley, the best-known bookseller and publisher in London. It was Dodsley who agreed to take on publication of *The Library*. The poem was published anonymously, but given Dodsley's pre-eminence most of London literary life was soon in the know about its authorship. From penurious obscurity Crabbe was quite suddenly transformed into a named poet, protégé of one of the great men of the age, and therefore someone to be taken seriously.

Still, while that promised much, such patronage did not guarantee money in his pocket. For that he needed further patronage. Again, Burke supplied it. He introduced Crabbe to the Duke of Rutland, and whispered in the poet's ear that he should look for modest preferment through the church. By the end of the year, therefore, Crabbe had been ordained as a Deacon and was briefly back in Aldeburgh as a curate. From there, ordained as a priest, he moved in 1782 to become personal chaplain to the Duke of Rutland at Belvoir Castle. His personal circumstances were now assured.

Meanwhile, what of *The Library*? As was common with long narrative poems of the period, Crabbe sets out 'The Argument' in order to let readers know what to expect.

Books offer Consolation to the troubled Mind by substituting a lighter kind of Distress for its own – They are productive of other Advantages – An Author's Hope of being known in distant times – Arrangement of the Library – Size and Form of the Volumes – The ancient Folio, clasped and chained – Fashion prevalent even in this Place – The Mode of publishing in Numbers, Pamphlets, &. – Subjects of the different Classes – Divinity – Controversy – The Friends of Religion often more dangerous than her Foes – Sceptical Authors – Reason too much rejected by the former Converts; exclusively relied upon by the latter – Philosophy ascending through the Scale of Being to Moral Subjects – Books of Medicine: their Variety, Varience, and Proneness to System: the Evil of this, and the Difficulty it causes – Farewell to this Study – Law: the increasing Number of its Volumes – supposed happy State of Man without Laws – Progress of Society – Historians: their Subjects – Dramatic Authors, Tragic and Comic – Ancient Romances – the Captive Heroine – Happiness in the perusal of such Books: why – Criticism – Apprehensions of the Author: removed by the Appearance of the Genius of the Place; whose reasoning and Admonition conclude the subject.

Towards the end of the poem, Crabbe addresses himself to the fate of any man 'who builds his peace of mind/On the precarious mercy of mankind', or who in his imagination envisages accomplishing great deeds or, perhaps, astounding feats of authorship. Such a man is almost certainly doomed to failure. The sentiments, even the cadences, are reminiscent of Johnson's remark that 'Human life is a condition in which much is to be endured and little enjoyed'. But relief, for the fortunate few at least, is at hand. Crabbe extols

Some generous friend of ample power possessed;
Some feeling heart, that bleeds for the distressed;
Some breast that glows with virtues all divine;
Some noble RUTLAND. Misery's friend and thine.

Benevolence was a widely-praised virtue of the century, perhaps because it was in short supply. Benevolence was what was expected of Men of Power, of affluence and influence. *Noblesse oblige.* This rather cringe-making praise of Rutland, which would be even more unctuous in the best of his early poems, *The Village*, is here presumably connected to his perusal of the library at Belvoir Castle, with which Crabbe, as the Duke's chaplain, was familiar by the time the poem had been completed in June, 1781.

But the poem isn't intended to provide an exact inventory of Rutland's holdings. The Library Crabbe describes is of a kind that was becoming increasingly familiar in towns and cities, especially in the midlands and north, in the later years of the eighteenth century. 'Subscription Libraries' they were called, and the subscribers were for the most part men who came together to form Literary and Philosophical Societies, who met regularly to discuss ideas and topics of the day; and who were alert to discoveries in astronomy, botany, geology, chemistry, as well as well-informed about the liberal arts – music, literature, drama, painting, sculpture, architecture. As 'The Argument' makes plain, Crabbe knows at least something about these and related subjects, and as the poem itself shows, he is also of his time in thinking that its especial virtues were largely due to the advancement of Learning.

Such Learning was furthered by the book trade. Publishers could supply works on all the issues that attracted the attention of subscribers. Authorship, bookshops, publishers, and libraries, were joined together in this new world of supply and demand. There is not much to be gained by arguing that *The*

Library is a poem we could not do without, but this much at least can be said for it, that over most of its length Crabbe shows himself well able to handle the couplet form competently, if not very adventurously; and that the subject itself shows that he is already developing the social awareness that will be intrinsic to the matter of many of his great poems. The private library – whether the possession of a gentleman or paid for by subscription – is a phenomenon of some importance in the later years of the eighteenth century.

It is typical of Crabbe to have sensed this and chosen it therefore as a subject well suited to his concerns. Earlier in the century a number of latter-day Georgics had found some favour with the reading public. Poems such as Dyer's *The Fleece*, *The Hop Field* by Christopher Smart, and Grainger's *The Sugar Cane*, provided a kind of Virgilian descriptive-cum-instructional exercise in poetic didacticism. You read them in order to learn from them. They provide what Mr Squeers called practical knowledge. 'When we've learnt how to spell winder we goes and cleans it'. In one sense Crabbe's poem is also didactic. Its account of what is contained within the library provides a perfectly good example of what *ought* to be in such a library. You could stock your own library from it. But the poem is not so much a Georgic, which after all has to do with recommendations and instructions for farmers, as a descriptive exercise which deals for the first time with what will become a staple element in Crabbe's work: household possessions and domestic arrangements. Moreover, it is alert to the widening interest in the life of the mind which is so remarkable a feature of the period and for which the possession of a library is the necessary prerequisite.

In the Verses he had written to promote his friend Garrick's taking control at Drury Lane, Johnson announced that 'When Learning's triumph o'er her barbarous foes/First rear'd the stage, Immortal Shakespeare rose'. In 'The Library', Crabbe rather echoes this sentiment in decrying a past time when 'by slow degrees the arts arose,/And Science waken'd from her long repose'. But this is not hyperbole. The eighteenth century was without doubt remarkable for the number of men, and sometimes women, of science who, from Newton on, created between them what Richard Holmes has called in a book of the same name, 'The Age of Wonder'.

The Age of Wonder was created both by outstanding individuals, natural scientists and observers, and by the coming together of those interested in, and knowledgeable about, the natural sciences. They formed clubs and societies, the most famous of which was the Lunar Society. This took its name from the fact that members regularly met on nights of a full moon, which made travelling from various midland cities to Birmingham, their customary meeting place, easier. The Lunar Men included among their members the chemist, Joseph Priestley, the Scottish engineer, James Watt, and a number of men seriously interested in, and informed about, geology, astronomy, anatomy, biology, and botany.

Priestley and Watt were famous. Other men of science in the latter half of the eighteenth century became equally well known, even famous. Joseph Banks was one. Banks, who eventually became president of the Royal Society (for the Advancement of Science), became something of a celebrity after his explorations of the southern seas – by means of Cook's Endeavour – resulted in the bringing home of many exotic plants and flowers as well as, in 1770, the famous Tahitian 'Omai', who became a celebrity in his own right in London for the following seven years, especially when he greeted George III with the words 'How do, King Tosh' – after which he returned to Tahiti. Another was the astronomer, Herschel, who, with his sister's assistance, built a telescope capable of discovering planets never before seen. Humphry Davy, whose experiments with gases led to the discovery of nitrous oxide as an anaesthetic, drew large audiences to his lectures. And there were others, all of whom gave a new authority to science, as well as introducing a sense not merely of wonder but nervous trepidation about the potential power of science to change the world. Hence, of course, Mary Shelley's *Frankenstein*.

In his own modest way Crabbe may be said to have contributed to this age of wonder. We know that soon after he moved to London in 1780 he became acquainted with a number of mathematicians and scientists, including the astronomer, John Bonnycastle, Isaac Dalby, and one-time president of the Royal Society, Reuben Burrow. We also know that at some stage he began the serious study of Latin in order to be able to present a botanical treatise on the flora of East Anglia. He did so because, following the taxonomy of plants established by the Swedish botanist, Linnaeus, it was taken for granted that all botanical work should be written in Latin. Crabbe had obviously not got far enough with his studies when, in 1796, he burnt a descriptive account of his native flora after being informed by John Davies, Vice-Master of Trinity College, Cambridge, that as he had written it in English it was worthless.

Nevertheless, he took these studies seriously. Like other Anglican vicars, above all Gilbert White, whose *Natural History of Selborne* was first published in 1789 and has never since been out of print, Crabbe saw himself as charged with recording at least some of nature's wonders. 'God moves in a mysterious way,/His wonders to perform.' The opening lines of the famous hymn by Crabbe's older contemporary, William Cowper (1731-1800) recognise how wonderfully strange nature's ways are. This is no longer a universe of Design, in which God is, as the French philosopher Malebranche had suggested, like a watchmaker, keeping the world ticking over according to regular and recognisable rules. In Cowper's words, God 'plants his footsteps in the sea/And rides upon the storm.' The world is altogether stranger, more mysterious, more tumultuous, than those who had argued for its evident orderliness could account for. Which brings us to the poem that established Crabbe's reputation.

III

The Village, published in 1783, was the first of Crabbe's full-length works to identify the author's name. It was published by Dodsley and was known to have been approved of by Samuel Johnson, who was shown the manuscript by Burke and who not merely emended it but re-wrote some lines near the beginning of the poem. *The Village* opens with the candid avowal not to pander to sentimental accounts of rural life. The times are altered, Crabbe says, though regrettably some poets cling to an out-dated pastoral mode, one that looks back to a Virgilian lyricism.

> Still in our lays fond Corydons complain,
> And shepherd boys their amorous pains reveal,
> *The only pains, alas! They never feel.*

Then he, or rather he and Johnson, continue

> On Mincio's banks, in Caesar's bounteous reign,
> If TITYRUS found the golden age again,
> Must sleepy bards the flattering dream prolong,
> Mechanic echoes of the Mantuan song?
> From truth and nature shall we widely stray,
> Where VIRGIL, not where fancy leads the way?

Showing off his awareness of Virgil (aka Tityrus) as the founder of literary pastoralism, Crabbe gets into a muddle from which Johnson cannot rescue him. In the eighteenth century the

31

Greek pastoral poet, Theocritus, was widely taken to be a kind of primitive. The nature and rural life he depicted were red in tooth and claw and decidedly hairy. Theocritus, in short, is being recruited for the debate about Originality versus Learning. He is an original genius, a true 'Goth'. Virgil, on the other hand, in both his *Eclogues* and *Georgics*, applied the sophistication of literary art to his writings about the rural life.

Crabbe wants to argue that Virgil was able to mythicise the pastoral life – re-discover the golden age – because of his great skill as an artist. But it's no good present-day poets trying to imitate this, he says. Wake up to the world. Confusingly, he also wants to assert that contemporary poets should be guided by Virgil because the great Roman master possesses both 'truth and nature'. There can be little doubt that Crabbe is here recalling some lines of Pope, who in his *Essay on Criticism* argued that Virgil learnt from Homer that the truest art lies in being true to nature.

> When first young Maro in his boundless mind,
> A work to outlast immortal Rome design'd,
> Perhaps he seemed above the Critic's Law,
> And but on Nature's fountain scorn'd to draw,
> But when to examine every part he came,
> Nature and Homer were, he found, the same.

Crabbe would have done better to have scrapped his own lines and cut straight to the chase. Because what he wants to do – at least in the First of the two Books that make up his poem – is to provide an unillusioned account of rural life that will decisively challenge the sentimental, soft-focus versions of pastoral common to the Picturesque convention.

The Picturesque had gained sufficient currency during the latter half of the eighteenth century to have imposed what amounted to a stylistic orthodoxy on both poetry and painting.

The Picturesque took for granted that landscape was best viewed from what was called a Prospect: that is, an appropriate vantage-point some distance off (a hill, or seat in a coach), that the best time of day to do the viewing was evening, because the drawing down of light invited a kind of genteel melancholy as well as providing a scene from which daily labourers had with luck disappeared – plodded homeward and left only the moping owl – that a ruined castle or cottage provided desirable constituents because they, too, inspired melancholy thoughts (the passage of time, the ancientness of the land, etc), and that nobody and nothing should be seen in close up. On the contrary, the Prospect required that *everything* surveyed should be caught in the haze of light which created an harmonious scene.

Travellers or connoisseurs of the Picturesque in late eighteenth-century England could take with them on their trips round the country (and Scotland and Wales) books by William Gilpin, who in a series of studies that are a kind of not-so-Rough Guides to Landscape, identified any number of Prospects which would afford Picturesque views. Naturally, these views excluded all that was unsightly. Gilpin was outraged when Arkwright's mill at Cromford interrupted a Picturesque view to which he was especially attached. There was nothing soothing, he complained in such evidence of industry, nothing to offer the viewer an atmosphere of reflective calm, of peace, even of plenitude, of nature's abundance.

Now consider this.

> Lo! Where the heath, with withering brake grown o'er,
> Lends the light turf that warms the neighbouring poor;
> From thence a length of burning sand appears,
> Where the thin harvest waves its withered ears;
> Rank weeds, that every art and care defy,
> Reign o'er the land and rob the blighted rye:
> There thistles stretch their prickly arms afar,

And to the ragged infant threaten war;
There poppies nodding, mock the hope of toil,
There the blue bugloss paints the sterile soil;
Hardy and high, above the slender sheaf,
The slimy mallow waves her silky leaf;
O'er the young shoot the charlock throws a shade,
And the wild tare clings round the sickly blade;
With mingled tints the rocky coasts abound,
And a sad splendour vainly shines around. (Book 1, lines 63-78)

From our vantage point in the early twenty-first century, it is perhaps difficult to grasp how extraordinary this writing is, how astonishing Crabbe's breakthrough, though some measure of his achievement can be gauged by reading such fine eighteenth-century landscape poems as Dyer's 'Grongar Hill' (1727), Gray's 'Elegy Written in a Country Churchyard' (1751) and, nearest to Crabbe's poem and perhaps the one he most instinctively challenges, Goldsmith's *The Deserted Village*. These are poems of individual distinction, two of them outstandingly so, but for all the differences between them the three can fairly be said to fall within the conventions of the Picturesque, though Goldsmith's radical challenge to its implicit politics is crucial to his poem's meaning.

Crabbe's poem by contrast, were it a candidate for acceptance as an example of Picturesque, would fail every test. We aren't looking from a distance, we aren't looking down on the scene, we aren't given a general 'harmonious' landscape, one which invites a pleasing nostalgia for a lost, golden age, and although at the end of the passage the perspective shifts from what feels restless eye-movement – the repeated 'There' acts as a kind of swivel pointing us in different directions – to allow a view of coastline, the 'mingled tints' provide, not a hazy outline of sea and shore, but an inhospitable rockiness lit by a 'sad splendour' – the only hint of picturesque – which emphasises discomfort.

A few lines later, Crabbe introduces humans into the scene:

> Here joyless roam a wild amphibious race,
> With sullen woe displayed in every face;
> Who far from civil arts and social fly,
> And scowl at strangers with suspicious eye.

Even if it's said, as quite a few commentators *do* say, that Crabbe is over-egging the pudding here, that the insistence on joylessness and lawlessness feels excessive, it has at least to be accepted that his linking of social circumstance with temperament is as persuasive as the 'golden' view of a contented peasantry promoted in *The Deserted Village*, to which, as I have already suggested, Crabbe's poem is very evidently a rejoinder. And you only have to think of Orlick in *Great Expectations* to recognise that Dickens, who had read Crabbe with great attentiveness, owes a debt to the poet in his creation of that murderous outsider, skulking around the Essex marshes on his own.

But it is Crabbe's detailed writing about the plants which inhabit his flat, featureless landscape that perhaps most require our attention and not merely because they challenge the easy assumption of a rural life in which toil is rewarded with rich harvests and a kind of communal sense of God's bounty to all. Such an assumption feeds the tradition which has, if not its beginnings, then its most eloquent expression in Pope's 'Windsor-Forest' (1713), a superb, unashamed, almost triumphalist, celebration of England's emergence as an imperial power, in which the land is imaged as a place of fruitful contentment, 'Where Order in Variety we see,/And where, tho' all things differ, all agree.'

> Here in full light the russet Plains extend;
> There wrapt in Clouds the bluish hills ascend:
> Ev'n the wild Heath displays her Purple Dies, [Dyes]

And midst the Desert fruitful Fields arise,
That crown'd with tufted Trees and springing Corn,
Like verdant Isles the sable Waste adorn.

Wherever you turn your eyes – Here/There – you will see that
'Rich Industry sits smiling on the Plains.' In such a land, nature's
God can predict that 'Safe on my Shore each unmolested
Swain/Shall tend the Flocks, or reap the bearded Grain.'

Admirer of Pope though he was, the Rev Crabbe is not
about to thank the Lord for extending His almighty hand in
order to feed and water *this* land. But then, much had
happened between Pope's announcement that 'Peace and
Plenty tell a Stuart Reigns', and the moment of *The Village*, and
not merely because by the time Crabbe wrote his poem the
Hanoverian dynasty had succeeded to the throne. I don't even
think Crabbe was much bothered about offering a corrective
vision to Pope's ecstatic account of England as a new Roman
Empire. It is more that, coming from unprivileged family
circumstances and growing up in a harsh environment, the
poet wasn't prepared to indulge a soft-focus account of the
natural world nor the people who lived there. As a result, *The
Village* is in every respect anti-pastoralist.

In the first place, nature's orderliness is turned upside down.
It is the rank weeds which 'reign o'er the land'. The weeds are
in control. As I have pointed out in my monograph on John
Clare (1994), the word 'weed' has no botanical meaning. It
simply means a plant growing where it isn't wanted. It is an
intruder, a pest, a threat to good order. The metaphoric
implication runs just under the surface here. Weeds are like the
hoi polloi, the plebs, the common people, threatening to infest
and ruin the orderly state.

They are moreover 'Rank'. It is a laden word. In his *Dictionary
of the English Language* (which Crabbe will certainly have
consulted), Johnson gives seven different meanings of the

adjective, six of which are relevant. Rank is 'High growing; strong; luxuriant'; it is 'Fruitful; bearing strong plants'; it is 'Strong smelling; rancid'; it is 'high tasted; strong in quality'; it is 'rampant; highgrown'; and it is 'gross; coarse'. We might also note that as a noun 'Rank' can mean a 'line of men placed a-breast', 'a range of subordination', and 'Class; order'. Exactly how much weight we give to these meanings isn't something that can be decided once and for all. What matters is that Crabbe's dark, laconic wit makes us recognise that the rank weeds decisively rob more than the blighted rye of an orderly fruitfulness.

So do the prickly thistles as they 'threaten war' to an infant whose ragged clothes dispel any hint of childish prettiness. (Compare the many paintings of well-dressed children to be found in eighteenth-century art, the setting often a garden or well-tended fields in which they gambol or are at ease in their mother's arms.) The nodding poppies – asleep like Biblical lazy tares? – drugged by their own fumes? – which mock the hope of toil, also indicate that this is not fruitful but 'sterile' soil, in which rank weeds alone flourish. Blue bugloss may be the forget-me-not, but in his *Englishman's Flora*, poet and formidable botanist, Geoffrey Grigson, links it to 'Scorpion Grass', which grows from six to twelve inches tall, and whose flowers here serve to light up the 'sterile soil' – where precious little else will grow.

Except, that is, for the mallow, 'slimy', Crabbe says, and according to Grigson, who is more forgiving, 'a species of waste and wayside', and the charlock, which the same writer characterises as 'a plant with a rat's individuality and lack of charm, although young wheatfields yellow with Charlock are among the undeniable pleasures of landscape.' To the wanderer, that is. The farmer takes a different view, especially given the plant's capacity for survival. 'Plough the old grass, and up comes the Charlock, like a vegetable rat.' And like the mallow, waving its silky leaf as if it were a banner fluttering victoriously above the new corn, so the charlock, throwing a shade over 'the young shoot', looms like death.

Wordsworth's objection to Crabbe's poetry being too full of matter-of-fact might look to vindication in the passage I have spent some time on. My own view is that the poetry lies precisely in the facts. Or rather, it is in the way Crabbe uses those facts to summon up a sense of the ceaseless – and losing – battle the toilers of the land fight against nature. The images of war, are after all, not fanciful, but derived from the plants' features and their proclivities. And the couplets are themselves marshalled in such a way as to provide a cumulative, remorseless sense of defeat for those wanting to subdue wild nature. 'And the wild tare clings round the sickly blade' – not literally sickly, of course, but the phrase suggests that those trying to wield weapons against their enemy are being overwhelmed.

In view of all this, Crabbe is entitled to the scorn of his questioning the pastoral tradition of poetry when, a little later, he enquires

> Ye gentle souls who dream of rural ease,
> Whom the smooth stream and smoother sonnet please;
> Go! If the peaceful cot your praises share,
> Go look within, and ask if peace be there:
> If peace be his – that drooping weary sire
> Or theirs, that offspring round their feeble fire,
> Or hers, that matron pale, whose trembling hand
> Turns on the wretched hearth the expiring brand.
>
> (lines 174-180)

As with the earlier passage, this has a particularity that contrasts with the distant view favoured by the Picturesque. There, the cottage is literally looked down on from the chosen viewing-point – the Prospect – and can be subsumed into a general account of a peaceful landscape. Thatched roof, smoke rising from the chimney – a peaceful cot. But in *The Village* we 'look within', and what we see rebukes the complacent account of rural peace and plenty that goes with the conventions of pastoralism.

'What's he know of the distresses of the poor musing over a snug coal fire in his parsonage box,' Clare asked rhetorically of Crabbe in a letter he wrote in 1820 to his own publisher. The answer is, he knew a lot, and what he knew he put for the first time into *The Village*. Nor was it merely a first for him. There's little in English poetry to anticipate the strong realism of Crabbe's poem about rural circumstance.

But he has a problem. Go back to the poem's opening and we get some inkling of Crabbe's difficulties. Crabbe wanted to tell the unvarnished truth about the rural poor. He is intent, so the prefatory lines make plain, on revealing more than the amorous pains of shepherd boys. He won't be content with prolonging 'the flattering dream' of rural ease. No extolling contemporary reality as a Golden Age, thank you very much. Faced with the lines about the hard, unremitting, and on the whole cheerless life of the agricultural poor, whether in the fields or at home, Clare could hardly complain that Crabbe was ignoring 'the distresses of the poor'.

But he could certainly have pointed to the following lines as vindication for his criticism.

> And you, ye poor, who still lament your fate,
> Forbear to envy those you reckon great;
> And know, amid those blessings they possess,
> They are, like you, the victims of distress;
> While Sloth with many a pang torments her slave,
> Fear waits on guilt, and Danger shakes the brave.

These lines (99-104) from Book Two of *The Village* seem to weasel their way out of what the poet himself had confronted in Book One. There, he had written sympathetically, if sternly, about the poor; here, he turns to admonish them as from the pulpit. Pity the well off, you've no idea how they suffer. Why, idleness is a dreadful form of suffering, and the rich, too, feel guilt, and, worse, the bravest have to encounter danger which can be a real shaker. What on earth is Crabbe banging on about?

It gets worse.

> Oh! If in life one noble chief appears,
> Great in his name, while blooming in his years;
> Born to enjoy whate'er delights mankind,
> And yet to all you feel or fear resigned;
> Who gave up pleasures you could never share,
> For pain which you are seldom doomed to bear;
> If such there be, then let your murmurs cease,
> Think, think of him, and take your lot in peace.

(lines 105-112)

Think of him? Think of *whom?* Who is this paragon of virtue who chose to give up pleasures the poor could never share? The answer is, the younger brother of Crabbe's patron, the Duke of Rutland, Lord Robert Manners.

Crabbe knew which side his bread was buttered. Hence, the egregious praise of the very nobility which had done so much to make the lives of the rural poor intolerable. (The Rutlands would go on doing so, by the way. When the First World War began, the then Duke summoned his estate workers to Grantham, took their horses away from them, told them to volunteer or leave his service, left them to walk home – some had long distances to cover; and used his Whitehall contacts to ensure that his own son, who was briefly behind the lines in France, never saw active combat. So much for *Noblesse Oblige.*)

Well, Crabbe couldn't have known that. But not much suggests that the Rutland who for a while gave him his living was a paragon of gentlemanly virtues. In short, *The Village* is a broken-backed poem. Book One is original, compelling, and for the most part very well written. Book Two is for the most part tripe. Fortunately, Crabbe never again made the mistake of being beholden to a patron. (Though he wasn't above penning some fairly cringe-making epigraphs.) He stayed in the Duke's employ for some years, but he was soon clear of Belvoir Castle. In 1784 he moved to Stathern in Leicestershire, as a curate, then, five years later, having succeeded in becoming LL.B., he became vicar at Muston, again in Leicestershire. By then he had married Sarah Elmy (in 1783), had fathered a son, George, eventually to become his biographer, and Sarah would produce four children before 1797, all of whom died in infancy.

IV

This may explain why the only other published poem of Crabbe's before 1807 was *The Newspaper*, of 1785. He did, however, publish 'The Natural History of the Vale of Belvoir' in *Bibliotheca Topographica Britannia* (1790), the year in which he began to take opium – it was prescribed for vertigo. And we know that he wrote and burnt some novels at the urgent request of his wife, who, as the deaths of her infant children mounted, seems to have become progressively withdrawn and depressed.

As for *The Newspaper*, which has most unfairly received a kicking from the few critics who have bothered to read it, it is a great improvement on *The Library*. Here is 'The Argument'

> This is not a time favourable for Poetical Composition: and why – Newspapers enemies to Literature, and their general Influence – Their Numbers – the Sunday Monitor – Their general Character – their Effect upon Individuals – upon Society – in the Country – the

Village Freeholder – What Kind of Composition a Newspaper is; and the Amusement it affords; Of what Parts it is chiefly composed – Articles of Intelligence: Advertisements: the Stage: Quacks: Puffing – The Correspondents to a Newspaper, political and poetical – Advice to the latter – Conclusion.

The opening feels pedestrian, the grouse against newspapers usurping an interest in true literature merely routine – why, after all, can't readers be interested in both? – but Crabbe hits his stride once he begins to spell out in some detail elements in newspapers he finds worthy of comment. Yes, newspapers are liable to be at the service of one political party or another, but this doesn't necessarily make them lickspittle sheets. Crabbe acknowledges the work of the printer H.S. Woodfull, who was prosecuted for allowing the famous Junius Papers to appear in his *Public Advertiser* for a five-year period between 1767 and 1772. They were then gathered together and published in book form a year later.

Nobody has ever claimed authorship of the Papers, which comprised vigorous attacks on Government ministers of the day, including the Dukes of Bedford and Grafton, and also made forceful criticisms of George III. Whoever wrote them clearly knew much about the inner workings of government, and their appearance in Woodfull's newspaper aroused much interest.

As Crabbe acknowledges, perhaps with Woodfull's publications in mind, the significance of newspapers is that 'within a single sheet,/Great things and small, the mean and mighty meet.' ''Tis this,' he adds, 'which makes all Europe's business known,/ Yet here a private man may place his own' – information, that is. For newspapers carry advertisements as well as news, and therefore where the private man reads 'of Lords and Commons, he/May tells their honours that he sells rapee.' (Rapee is a dialect version of 'rape wine', made from the stalks and refuse of grapes, with water added.) 'All Europe's news' is excessive. There were, after all, no foreign correspondents, and this was an age when Jane Austen's father found himself called on to settle a dispute between two farmers as to whether France was the capital of Paris, or Paris the capital of France.

But Crabbe is fascinated by the way in which a newspaper acts as an *omnium gatherum* for both the grave and the trivial, similar to the manner in which the Turkish novelist, Orhun Pamuck, describes the amateur encyclopaedias of his native Istanbul, where any material, from the most serious to the least important, is allotted space. Hence, the following lines, where Crabbe, however sardonically, acknowledges a newspaper's appeal to a wide variety of readers.

> Grave politicians look for facts alone,
> And gravely add conjectures of their own;
> The sprightly nymph, who never broke her rest
> For tottering crowns or mighty lands oppressed,
> Finds broils and battles, but neglects them all
> For songs and suits, a birthday and a ball:
> The keen, warm man o'erlooks each idle tale
> For 'Monies wanted' and 'Estates on Sale';
> While some with equal minds to all attend,
> Pleased with each part, and grieved to find an end.

'Songs and suits, a birthday and a ball'. Newspapers carried announcements of social events as well as printing poems by their readers. Regional and local ones still do.

But something else needs here to be noted. Look at Crabbe's handling of narrative couplets, consider his ability to let a sentence run over ten lines with the rhymes pushing forward what he has to say, rather than containing statements within the tight couplet form he had for the most part previously worked with. He is learning to tell a story.

This is of some importance. Of equal importance is the fact that the story Crabbe has to tell here is rooted in daily life. *The Rape of the Lock*, Pope's wondrous, near baroque tale of the 'dire causes' that arise from 'amorous things', tells the story of one young girl who is put out of temper because a beau clips a ringlet of her hair and so disturbs the universe. 'Calm were the waves, the zephyrs gently play,/Belinda smiled and all the World was gay.' But gaiety vanishes once the heinous act is done. Pope's exuberant satire is aimed at the absurd vanity of those who inhabit the tiny, fashionable 'world' of early eighteenth-century London and who think their lives of truly world-shaking significance.

Crabbe, on the other hand, admirer of Pope though he was, is writing about a very different world: the non-metropolitan populace, or of that section which stretches from the poor to the comfortably-off middle class. This is a wide range of English people, more than had been written about by English poets, at least since Chaucer. To be sure, Shakespeare had covered such a range, and more beside. And by the time Crabbe began to write English novelists were taking as subject matter what might be called the common people. The English novel comes into its own in the eighteenth century largely because of the existence of people who were newly able to spend time and money (books could be expensive) on reading, and for whom prose fiction became a desideratum because in the pages of Defoe, Fielding, Richardson, Smollett, and others, they could find themselves reading about characters like themselves. Fiction in a sense reflected their lives, often distorted or exaggerated, but nevertheless recognisable. Fiction made its readers visible to themselves and each other.

But until Crabbe, no poet had written about what is in fact an emerging kind of Englishness, often, though not always, property-owning, literate but not usually university-educated, farmers, tradesmen, lawyers, bankers, some newly rich, others newly respectable, still others clinging to fading notions of grandeur, members of the squirearchy, clergymen, apothecaries, military men, sailors, country justices, magistrates, doctors ...

The range is extraordinary and helps to explain, I think, why the great English novelists of the nineteenth century so admired Crabbe. And for all its occasional longeurs, *The Newspaper* is the first poem in which Crabbe announces himself as the poet of this Englishness, perhaps because a newspaper caters for a similar readership. As he says, in its pages you will find

> Deeds of all kinds, and comments to each deed.
> Here stocks, the state barometers, we view,
> That rise or fall by causes known to few;
> Promotion's ladder who goes up and down,
> Who wed, or who seduced amuse the town;
> What new-born heir has made his father blest;
> What heir exults, his father now at rest ...

The 'town' doesn't have to be London. It could as well be Bristol or Norwich or Nottingham, all of which acquired newspapers during this period. And though when Crabbe comes to write some lines on 'puffing' – that is, the promoting in newspaper columns of books and plays by hacks hired by the publisher or theatre owner – he has London in his sights, other forms of 'puffery' are more widely distributed among cities and country towns, as with 'barbers' boys, who would in trade advance', and who therefore 'Wish us to call them smart Friseurs from France', or 'he who builds a chop-house' and who 'on his door/Paints "The true old original Blue Boar"'. Clearly those ludicrous signs announcing 'The Olde Sweete Shoppe', etc didn't spring newly from the brain of some mid-twentieth-century marketing consultant.

Though, to repeat, Wordsworth might complain that the

Muse had nothing to do with Crabbe's reporting 'mere matters of fact', Crabbe was proving himself the willing and able servant of a new kind of muse, one in which social observation, blended with a strong and typically dark comedic element, made him, as Byron would claim, Nature's sternest painter and her best – by which Byron didn't mean a painter merely of landscapes, though Crabbe would certainly prove to be that, too.

3

Re-emergence poems

I

Between 1785 and 1807 Crabbe published no new poetry. This twenty-two-year gap isn't entirely barren of publications. As already mentioned, there were in particular two essays reflective of his interest in flora and fauna. The first, 'The Natural History of the Vale of Belvoir', appeared in 1790 in Nichols' *Bibliotheca Topographica Brittanica*, and eight years later he contributed 'A Catalogue of Plants growing in and near the parish of Framlingham' to Hawes and Loder's *History of Framlingham*. But these were minor works. Two years earlier, he had been frustrated in his ambition to publish a detailed treatise on botanical classification, especially as it affected the plants of East Anglia, when the Vice-Master of Trinity College, Cambridge, told him that such a work, written as it was in English, would be unacceptable to its intended readership. Presumably anyone not a Latinist couldn't be expected to have a serious interest in botany. Not all was lost, however. From now on, as we shall see, Crabbe would make use of his extensive botanical knowledge in footnotes he supplied to poems whenever they seemed at all relevant.

But it seems plain enough that the years between the publication of *The Newspaper* and 1807, when the sizeable *Poems* appeared, were difficult ones. Because I am not writing a biography, what follows is the merest outline, but it will, I hope, be sufficient to explain that although Crabbe's emergence from the life of humdrum apothecary and failed scribbler was in some ways a success story, it wouldn't necessarily have felt like that. George Orwell once said that judged from the inside every life seems a failure, and there seems no reason to exempt Crabbe from Orwell's sobering judgement. He doesn't seem to have been at ease with his pastoral duties, and his frequent moves from one parish to another weren't calculated to endear him to his congregations.

Nor did they. He went from Strathern, where he had become curate in 1784, to the living of Muston in 1789, two years later moved to Parham, in Lincolnshire, moved again in 1796 and then again in 1801, and only returned to Muston, of which he was still vicar, in 1806, when, so Edwards says, 'Laws against absentee clergy demanded his return.' When he finally left that living in 1814 the villagers turned out to ring the church bells in a show of celebration.

And the Crabbes' home life had its chills and fevers. After the deaths in infancy of four of her children in the 1790s, Sarah fell into a prolonged depression. In his biographical account, Crabbe junior hints that his mother's mental state was exacerbated by a gloomy conviction of unworthiness, of God's punishment. Hence Crabbe's decision at the start of the new century to destroy no fewer than three novels, all of which seem to have been completed. He was complying with the wishes of a wife who, influenced by her religious beliefs, saw fiction as corrupt and corrupting.

By then he himself was addicted to the opium which he had first been prescribed in 1790. Opium, or laudanum – a tincture of opium often taken in liquid form – was the fashionable medicine of its day, recommended for a wide variety of ailments, from sleeplessness, through the vertigo which plagued Crabbe, to 'low spirits'. Opium was the Valium and Prozac of its day. To continue to be effective, it also had to be taken in increasingly strong doses, and with that came side effects, in particular disturbing dreams. De Quincey and Coleridge were among the distinguished contemporaries of

Crabbe who suffered from such dreams, and commentators have suggested that the dreams which afflict the protagonist of Crabbe's poem, 'Sir Eustace Grey' read very much as though they are opium fuelled.

Perhaps for this reason, the poem, which may have been written in the winter of 1804-5, and which was published in the 1807 *Poems*, has received much favourable comment. During Crabbe's lifetime it was probably the most popular of his poems, and along with 'The Hall of Justice' it prompted the critic Francis Jeffrey, when reviewing *Poems* in the influential *Edinburgh Review*, to call Crabbe 'one of the most original, nervous, and pathetic poets of the present century.' In making this claim, Jeffrey was taking aim at the Lake poets, Wordsworth especially, for whom he had little time. According to Jeffrey, the Lake poets 'show us something that mere observation never yet suggested to anyone.' They are immune to 'mere matters of fact'. He did not approve of 'the light that never was on sea or land'.

In his generously enthusiastic review of Crabbe's new book, Jeffrey directs especial praise at two ballad-like poems. 'The Hall of Justice', written mostly in quatrains, consists of a dialogue between a magistrate called upon to try and sentence a woman guilty of theft, and the woman herself, who has a tale to tell of seduction, betrayal, unavoidable wandering with a gipsy gang, abandonment, marriage to a man who forces her into prostitution, further abandonment, near starvation, and, eventually, and pathetically, a re-uniting with her daughter before that daughter's transportation, while she herself is left with the daughter's infant child, another daughter. It is for her she steals, and the Magistrate, who by the end of the poem seems to have turned priest, brings her to voice her repentance for her crime, at which point she is freed.

I can see why contemporaries would have been affected by the poem. When Jeffrey called Crabbe 'nervous' he didn't mean he was timorous but that he was full-nerved, vigorous; that he wasn't a namby pamby. 'The Hall of Justice', as well as being 'pathetic' – that is, emotionally affecting – also presents a strong story in which a life of unjustified hardship is not so much gloomed over as given with a degree of frankness which has no room for sentimentality. In *this* sense it is 'nervous'. But the ending, in which the Magistrate tells the vagrant woman that she will know she has been redeemed when she can say '"MY SAVIOUR, I REPENT!"', is less likely to appeal to modern readers, not because the upholder of the Law can be accused of complacency – that's the kind of conventional thing he would say – but because Crabbe can. The poem, that is, endorses the propriety of the magistrate's point of view. And we have then to reflect that Jeffrey, for all his Whig, reformist sympathies, would have been far less challenged by Crabbe's innate conservatism than by what, at that time, were Wordsworth's more radical politics.

Crabbe, the country clergyman with strong Johnsonian propensities, seems always to have endorsed or taken for granted the desirability of the social status quo and of the need for moderation in behaviour, thought, and ethics. 'Sir Eustace Grey', the other poem Jeffrey makes much of, is a cautionary tale about what can happen to a mind that lets itself be overthrown by excess.

> Scene – A MADHOUSE
> Persons: VISITOR, PHYSICIAN, AND PATIENT
> Veris miscens falsa. –
> SENECA in Herc. furente

This is how the introduction to the poem is set out. The epigraph, 'mixing true and false' is from Seneca's famous play about the mad Hercules, a drama often cited in the eighteenth century as an instructive instance of the need for restraint, for moderation in all things. Visits to madhouses were common practice during the period, and there is a whole literature about how insanity in its various manifestations was at the time identified, accounted for, and treated. Of these, probably still the best is Roy Porter's *Madmen: A Social History of Madhouses, Mad-Doctors, & Lunatics* (2006 – originally published in 1987 as *Mind-Forg'd Manacles*). Porter doesn't mention Crabbe, though he discusses such contemporaries as Christopher Smart, Blake, Cowper and Coleridge, and he spends a whole chapter on 'Confinement and its Rationales', of which the Madhouse which confines Sir Eustace is an example.

Crabbe's poem is about a man of wealth and family who falls mad after he discovers his wife is having an affair with his friend, kills the friend; he is then immured in the madhouse, 'The sport of Madness, Misery's prey'. The poem is for the most part written in a stanza form that can be called a 'literary ballad', in some ways reminiscent of Wordsworth's 'The Thorn' – to take a random instance – although there are many other examples that could be cited. For during the period that coincides with Crabbe's early years, poets were experimenting with forms that could free them from what they thought of as the shackles of the heroic couplet, especially as that was associated with an outworn politics and social vision: of containment, refinement, of a classical heritage associated with Augustan Rome. To return to a subject I raised in the previous chapter, the rise of 'Gothic', of a deliberate cultivation of the 'barbaric', of elevating originality above 'school' learning, inevitably brought with it an interest in ballad forms as expressions of native utterance. Ballads were the songs of the people. And it isn't difficult to see how this kind of *vox. pop.* would find favour among poets whose radicalism inevitably led to a more democratising sense of the constituency for poetry.

What is more difficult to see is why this might affect Crabbe who was, as I say, a man of conservative instincts and convictions. But then 'Sir Eustace Grey' is hardly a ballad of the

kind we can call 'popular'. Here is Sir Eustace describing his
own former and greatly favoured self.

> Yes! I had youth and rosy Health;
> Was nobly formed, as Man might be;
>   For sickness then, of all my Wealth,
> I never gave a single Fee:
>   The Ladies fair, the Maidens free,
> Were all accustomed then to say,
>   Who would a handsome Figure see,
> Should look upon Sir Eustace Grey.

But later, after the flight of his wife and her lover, the killing of
his rival, and the deaths, first of his wife and then of his three
children, Grey falls into the madness that leads to his
confinement. Why it didn't lead to the gallows isn't explained,
but undoubtedly has to do with the fact that it was easier for
those with titles to escape the full rigours of the law. Sir Eustace
tells the visitor of his frightful night visions, of how he is
whirled about the universe by 'commissioned Foes' – evil spirits
– who fixed him 'upon a shaking Fen', then 'hung me on a
Bough, so small,/The Rook could build her nest no higher', and
because of whom 'I've hung upon the ridgy Steep/Of Cliffs,
and held the rambling Briar;/I've plunged below the billowy
Deep … I've made the Badger's Hole my bed … I've wandered
with a Gipsy Crew', and much more beside. Vertigo feeds into
these nightmare visions, so, too, fear of being a social outcast.
    The upshot of it all is that Grey becomes

> A Soul defiled with every Stain,
> That Man's reflecting Mind can pain;
>   That Pride, Wrong, Rage, Despair can make,
> In fact, they'd nearly touched my Brain,
>   And Reason on her Throne would shake.

'Nearly' here doesn't so much mean 'almost' as 'the nearest way'. Pride and the rest of them, Despair especially (the cardinal sin) have so got at Grey's brain/mind that he is close to losing his Reason.

Gradually, however, religious faith began to restore him, to form, so the Physician tells the Visitor, 'a frenzied Child of Grace'. But 'frenzied' indicates that this sort of religious conviction – 'enthusiasm' its opponents called it – is emotional rather than reasonable. And the Physican knows better than to believe that a permanent cure lies this way. The poem concludes with his words:

> But ah! Though Time can bring Relief,
>   And soften Woes it cannot cure;
> Would we not suffer Pain and Grief,
>   To have our Reason sound and sure?
> Then let us keep our bosoms pure,
>   Our Fancy's favourite Flights suppress;
> Prepare the Body to endure,
>   And bend the mind to meet Distress;
> And then his guardian Care implore,
>   Whom Demons dread and Men adore.

Lying in bed, gravely ill with dropsy, Johnson asked the physician who had come to visit him, 'Canst thou not minister to a mind diseased,/Pluck from the memory a rooted sorrow,/And with some sweet oblivious antidote,/Cleanse the stuff'd bosom of that perilous stuff/Which weighs upon the heart.' And the doctor, who knew his *Macbeth*, replied, apparently to Johnson's delight, 'Therein the patient/Must minister to himself'. Crabbe would almost certainly have known that story, which Boswell tells, because the great *Life of Samuel Johnson LL.D.* had been published in 1791. In which case he would also have known that Johnson said that 'human life is a condition in which much is to be endured and little enjoyed.'

My own view is that 'Sir Eustace Grey' is best understood, not as an exercise in Gothicry, but as a Johnsonian consideration of the need for restraint against the lures of excess. 'Enthusiasm' was one form of excess. It was especially identified with Methodism. The enthusiast was someone whose inner certainty of being the recipient of God's Grace was customarily linked to the conversion from 'heaviness' (conviction of being potentially damned) to 'joy'. According to his own journals, Wesley's preaching turned many in his congregations to joy from their previous heaviness. But to sceptical outsiders, such conversion, especially in its more 'enthusiastic' manifestation of what in the following century would sometimes be labelled hysteria, at all events if it was shown by a woman, might seem less evidence of God's grace than mental delusion. And what if conversion went the other way: from joy to heaviness? It hardly needs to be said that Crabbe might have considered he had a case of such dread conversion to hand in the depression that settled on his own wife. (For more on the effects of 'enthusiasm' see my essay 'The Poet in his Joy: Why and How a Word changed its meaning in the 18th century' in *Romantic to Modern: Essays* (1982).)

That Crabbe was deeply interested in 'the mind diseased' is obvious to any reader of 'Peter Grimes'; but time and again he is recalled to the Johnsonian gravitas so evident in the remark in *The History of Rasselas, Prince of Abyssinia* (1759), where Johnson has Imlac remark that 'Of the uncertainties of our present state, the most dreadful and alarming is the uncertain continuance of reason.' And for all that Crabbe may make use of a ballad form in this and other, later poems, with its four-stress line and interlaced rhymes, the literary ballad is part of the achievement of eighteenth-century poetry overall. In writing as he does, Crabbe is deliberately associating himself with the practice *and* convictions of his eighteenth-century forebears, above all, I think, Johnson, whose stoical quietism is behind Imlac's statement that 'All that virtue can afford is quietness of conscience, a steady prospect of a happier state; this may enable us to bear calamity with patience; but remember that patience must suppose pain.'

This could almost be the motto for 'Sir Eustace Grey.'

II

Imlac's words could also form a suitable motto for Jane Austen's work, above all, perhaps, *Persuasion*. Yet it was in an earlier novel, *Mansfield Park*, that the novelist used the name Fanny Price for her heroine and in so doing made a conscious bow in the direction of the poet she so admired that, having heard of the death of Crabbe's wife, she told her sister she could imagine herself as 'the second Mrs Crabbe'. Fanny Price is the name of a character who appears in 'Marriages', Part Two of *The Parish Register*, the major work of the 1807 *Poems*. Part One deals with 'Baptisms', Part Three with 'Burials', and between them all three parts survey what the narrating voice calls 'The simple Annals of my Parish poor'.

The voice is that of an Anglican vicar. It may not be Crabbe's, but any reader could be forgiven for assuming that there is not much to separate the person who narrates *The Parish Register* from the poet who wrote it. That the tone of this voice contains a degree of condescension may well explain why Clare was so irritated by what he thought of as Crabbe's 'ignorance' of the poor whose annals he claims to 'explore'. There's no doubt that Parson Crabbe occupies what might be called the Anglican middle ground. He is politically and socially conservative. He believes in a fixed order of things, is against excess from whichever quarter it comes; and the statements about religion that from time to time crop up in *The Parish Register* are in the tradition of the Dryden who had over a century earlier asserted in 'Religio Laici' that 'Points obscure are of small use to learn,/But common quiet is mankind's concern.' Religious factionalism – 'the private spirit' – was in Dryden's time the cause of civil unrest; and so it was in the early nineteenth century.

Hence, the following lines, which occur early on in 'Burials', where Crabbe, as I will call the narrator, surveys the reading matter of those he calls 'rustic readers'. *The Pilgrim's Progress* is sure to be an essential text, which is not necessarily a good thing. 'A genius rare but rude was honest John,' Crabbe remarks, 'Not one who, early by the Muse beguiled,/Drank from her well the water undefiled; / ... But one who dabbled in the sacred springs,/And drank them muddy, mixed with baser things'. Bunyan, the tinker, the man who roamed the country preaching his message of resistance to the Church's presumed authority, and who for his pains was imprisoned as a danger to peace, is still, the narrator here implies, a threat to common quiet. As are others who interpret the Bible according to their own lights. Rustic readers may well be misled by such interpreters who

> Have made them stop to reason why? and how?
> And where they once agreed, to cavil now.
> Oh! Rather give me commentators plain,
> Who with no deep researches vex the brain;
> Who from the dark and doubtful love to run,
> And hold their glimmering tapers to the sun;
> Who simple truth with nine-fold reason back,
> And guard the point no enemies attack.

Crabbe is here echoing the opening of Dryden's 'Religio Laici', where the light of reason is compared with religion's truth and reason's 'glimmering ray' found unequal to faith's 'supernatural light'. But why bother? Why appeal to a poem and a rhetoric that was by the time Crabbe was writing *The Parish Register* more than a hundred years old?

The answer is, that in the early years of the nineteenth century religious Dissent was growing apace among the rural as among the industrial poor. In 'The Hind and the Panther', written after his conversion to the Roman church, Dryden has the Hind, who speaks for his new church, reprove Anglicanism because for all its glittering beauty, it is like a faulty diamond: 'sparklets shattered into sects'. In the early nineteenth century new sects were everywhere. (Their traces can still be seen in the chapels and meeting rooms scattered among the back streets of towns and villages throughout England, larger ones now turned into car show-rooms or carpet warehouses, smaller buildings converted to private residences.) Crabbe himself came up against a group called 'The Huntingtonians', so-called because their leader was the coal heaver-turned preacher William Huntington S.S. (standing for 'Sinner Saved'.)

Dissent derived from interpretations of the bible which challenged official Anglicanism, or from Revelation. And there's no arguing with Revelation any more than reason can effectively oppose Joy. Crabbe may look to be on dangerous ground in opposing simple Faith to 'dark' Reason. Wasn't Reason precisely what he was supposed to prefer? But the point is that the Reason which he upholds is that which does *not* pry into difficult territory but which is, in Dryden's words, content to accept that 'The things we need to know are few and plain'. It is false reason, specious argumentation, which finds in the Bible the supposed authority for all kinds of challenges to Anglican reasonableness. And such challenges could and did include the justification for radical opposition to authority, whether religious or secular.

Not all the sects which formed under a declaration of Revelation were political in nature, but some, including the most powerful, were. To put it very simply: if the New Testament promised that the meek shall inherit the earth, why hadn't they? Why, as a later hymn would insist, did Anglicanism take for granted that 'The rich man at his castle,/The poor man at his gate,/God made them high and lowly,/And ordered their estate'? Surely it wasn't God who made this arrangement but the 'Tory party at prayer', as the Anglican church would be dubbed?

These and other questions, which E.P. Thompson raised in his classic account of *The Making of the English Working Class* (1963), helped to prompt the growth of Dissent in the years when Crabbe was writing. And it may be that 'snug in his parsonage box' Crabbe, while undoubtedly aware of the presence of Dissent, was indifferent to its legitimate causes. But he had certainly 'looked within' the cottages where the poor of the parish lived. He knew as well as Clare that among the reading matter likely to be found there were 'Crowns Thumb the Great, and Hickathrift the strong./There too is he, by wizard-power upheld,/Jack, by whose arm the giant-brood were quell'd'. (Compare Clare's much later sonnet, recalling from the asylum where he was immured, his own home life 'With lots of pictures and good stories too/And Jack the jiant killers high renown' ('To John Clare').

Besides, Crabbe doesn't in *The Parish Register* shirk the miseries of those who have to live in want, who struggle for survival in what we would call slum conditions. (But the word didn't then exist. He calls the place a 'Row' – a street of rotten houses.) In a passage too long to quote in full – it runs for some hundred and fifty lines – Crabbe details how 'Boys in their first-stoln rags, to swear begin, /And girls, who heed not dress, are skill'd in gin: /Snarers and smugglers here their gains divide; Ensnaring females here their victims hide: ... There lie, obscene, at every open door,/Heaps from the hearth, and sweepings from the floor,/And day by day the mingled masses grow,/As sinks are disembogued and kennels flow ... There dropsied infants wail without redress,/And all is want and woe and wretchedness.'

I know of nothing before Dickens' description of the London slums occupied by Fagin and his gang to equal Crabbe's account of the 'Row', and this is crucial. Because in this respect alone *The Parish Register* is doing something brand-new in English literature. Its focus on urban and rural living takes in, unsentimentally, a range of social experiences that no other poet had so much as touched on, let alone explored. Crabbe is the great realist of English poetry, if by this we mean, as we should, a writer who sees it as his responsibility to 'portray life with fidelity'. Crabbe's habitual use of the couplet has conventionally led to him being called a later Augustan. And his equally habitual concern with non-metropolitan life has prompted the jibe about him being 'Pope in worsted stockings'. But in the way he writes about that life he is a radical innovator. And *The Parish Register* is not only the first of his major works, but one which helps to explain why the great nineteenth centry novelists so intensely admired him, and why they took so much from his work.

Jane Austen has nothing to equal Crabbe's account of 'The Row'. The nearest she comes to is when she has Emma and Harriet Smith pay 'a charitable visit' to a 'poor sick family'. Emma, we are told, 'understood their ways, could allow for their ignorance and their temptations, had no romantic expectations of extraordinary virtue from those for whom education had done so little; entered into their troubles with ready sympathy; and always gave her assistance with as much intelligence as good-will'. And having done that, she and Harriet take their leave, allowing Emma to say ' "These are the sights, Harriet, to do one good. How trifling they make everything else appear! – I feel now as if I could think of nothing but these poor creatures all the rest of the day; and yet, who can say how soon it may all vanish from my mind?" ' (Vol. 1, ch. X) And sure enough, round a bend in the lane they meet Mr Elton, and the poor are forgotten.

This isn't a point to labour, but the complacency of this is not merely Emma's. Jane Austen skewers that, right enough, but we are told precisely nothing about the 'poor creatures' who so engage Emma's attention. What *are* their ways, what, for that matter, is the nature of the sickness and trouble that invites Emma's sympathy? But Jane Austen's attention is all on that famous 'two square inches of ivory'. Anglican vicar though (or because?) her father was, she herself doesn't in her fiction stray beyond the bounds of the middle-class provincial communities she studies with such merciless acuity.

And yet she had obviously read *The Parish Register*, because, to repeat, the Fanny Price of *Mansfield Park* is without doubt a bow in the direction of the Fanny Price about whom Crabbe writes in Part Two of his poem. Crabbe's Fanny Price is, like Jane Austen's heroine, 'lovely' and 'chaste', and both are the objects of desire of socially superior men, who offer marriage but sooner would settle for seduction. Crabbe's 'Sir Edward Archer is an amorous knight,/And maidens chaste and lovely shun his sight'. Fanny doesn't do this but she has no intention of surrendering to his blandishments. He tries flattery, telling her that, daughter of his bailiff though she may be, she shouldn't waste herself in marriage to a ploughman, not when he can supply her with 'The softest carpets ... Pictures of happiest love' (erotic prints, he probably means), and 'tallest mirrors' in which she can study herself by 'the hands of wealth and fashion dress'd'.

But he is wasting his time. Fanny tells him that her mother 'loved, was married, toil'd and died;/With joys she'd griefs, had troubles in her course;/But not one grief was pointed by remorse.' Archer, that Sagittarius of the boudoir, admits himself defeated, and so, rather as in the end Emma allows Harriet to marry the yeoman farmer Robert Martin rather than any 'superior' gentleman, so Sir Edward 'befriends a youth,/Who to the yielding maid had vow'd his truth', and, it is implied, welcomes their marriage. No upward social mobility there, then.

Many years ago, the American critic, Lionel Trilling, suggested that the marriage between Harriet Smith and Robert Martin in Austen's *Emma* emblematised a kind of social cement, a reconciliation between classes, which guaranteed that the revolutionary events shaking France couldn't happen here. This seems to me pie-in-the-sky. England, after all, came very close to such a revolution in 1839. It is more accurate, I think, to suggest that the Anglican conservatism, which Crabbe and Austen share, and which takes for granted social and class distinctions, also takes for granted civic responsibilities, including mutual tolerance and understanding between classes. This has a bearing on a key moment in Part Three of *The Parish Register*.

Here is Crabbe's account of the death of someone he identifies only by her title.

> Next die the LADY who yon Hall Possess'd,
> And here they brought her noble bones to rest.
> In Town she dwelt; – forsaken stood the Hall:
> Worms ate the floor, the tap'stry fled the wall:
> No fire the kitchen's cheerless grate display'd;
> No cheerful light the long-clos'd sash convey'd;
> The crawling worm, that turns a summer fly,
> Here spun his shroud and laid him up to die
> The winter death: – upon the bed of state
> The bat shrill-shrieking woo'd his flickering mate;
> To empty rooms the curious came no more;
> From empty cellars turn'd the angry poor,
> And surly beggars curs'd the ever-bolted door.
> To one small room the steward found his way
> Where tenants follow'd to complain and pay;
> Yet no complaint before the Lady came,
> The feeling servant spared the feeble dame;
> Who saw her farms with his observing eyes,
> And answer'd all requests with his replies; –

She came not down, her falling groves to view;
Why should she know what one so faithful knew?
Why come, from many clamorous tongues to hear
What one so just might whisper in her ear?
Her oaks or acres why with care explore;
Why learn the wants, the sufferings of the poor;
When one so knowing all their worth could trace,
And one so piteous govern'd in her place?
The Lady is buried with due ceremony.
Lo! Now, what dismal Sons of Darkness come,
To bear this Daughter of Indulgence home;
Tragedians all, and well-arranged in black,
Who nature, feeling, force, expression lack,
Who cause no tear but gloomily pass by,
And shake their sables in the wearied eye
That turns disgusted from the pompous scene ...

If this isn't marvellous writing I never writ nor no man ever loved. The account of the Lady's dereliction of duty is made with full awareness of the tradition of what is called the Country House Poem, one that survives at least as far as the 1960s, when Charles Tomlinson included in his collection, *Seeing is Believing*, his poem, 'On the Hall at Stowey', investing that particular country house with a symbolic history of responsible social relationship. 'Five centuries – here were (at the least) five – /In linked love', where 'the corn levelled' went with 'foison', that is a richness available to those who work the land quite as much as those who own it.

Clinging on to this questionable and, as years progress, grotesquely false, account of social relations, even if only to elegise it, is merely sentimental. Hence, 'History Lesson', a pastiche-poem I wrote some years after Tomlinson's, which ends with the ancient lord and lady of a manor being shot by 'levelling guns', and which has, as refrain, *And this is going to be how History stops./And this is going to be how history starts'*. By the middle of the nineteenth century, any account of English History with a capital H which tugged a forelock to the propriety of country-house politics was endorsing a frankly misleading image of social relations, one that ought to have been brought to an end far earlier. The fact is, that such deeply conservative politics, which sustain, for example, *Mansfield Park* and *Emma*, are increasingly at odds with actuality.

Jane Austen is to be exonerated from falsifying history at least to the extent that her country house is imaged as an ideal, something to be wished for. Others were less cautious. But asserting the continuing existence of the enriching and stabilising consequences which came from mutual respect between lord and peasantry, supposing it *ever* to have existed, is to turn your back on history. Dickens' *Bleak House* (1853), and, a generation later, Hardy's best novel, *The Woodlanders*, (1887), provide between them what might be thought of as definitive rebukes to the politics of Country House poetry.

In his account of the 'Lady of the Hall', Crabbe undoubtedly aligns himself with the tradition which places reliance on the good effects of the country house and its responsibilities. It is, of course, a development of the old Feudal ideal. The Lord owns the land, the peasants work on it. They offer him their labour, he offers them protection from harm. The upshot is social harmony. When the action in *The Merchant of Venice* moves in the last act from the mercantile and aggressive city to the settled calm of the house at Belmont, Portia, standing before her house, says 'That light we see is burning in the hall:/How far that little candle throws his beams!/So shines a good deed in a naughty world'. The light of the house, in this instance given off by a candle, is typically associated with household gods of peace and assured hospitality. In his great poem of 1611, 'To Penshurst', the country house of the Sidneys, Ben Jonson reports how 'King James, when hunting late, this way,/With his brave son, the prince, they saw thy fires/Shine bright on every hearth as the desires/Of thy Penates had been set on flame'. A grand compliment recruits the idea of Roman household gods who burn in the hearth to welcome visitors.

These visitors include the peasantry and others who work the land. The walls of Penshurst are for all: 'There's none, that dwell about them, wish them down;/But all come in, the farmer and the clown'. They do not come empty-handed but bring with them the produce of their toil, and in return for their gifts they receive hospitality from the lord of the house 'Whose liberal board doth flow,/With all, that hospitality doth know'.

As most commentators on Jonson's poem acknowledge, 'To Penshurst' is both endorsement of the country house ideal and, implicitly, an admission that for the most part the ideal is honoured in the breach. Goldsmith's *The Deserted Village*, written late in the following century, may celebrate the same ideal but is more candid in conveying how it has fallen into desuetude. Greed and selfishness are now far more typical of the landed gentry than any sense of responsibility to the land or those who work it. It is notable then that in the more than a century that divides the two poets, the noun 'pomp' and adjective 'pompous' change their meanings. The change comes most abruptly in the middle years of the eighteenth century. We can see this if we consult Johnson's *Dictionary* (1755), which gives the meaning of 'pomp' as 'Splendour; pride'; as for 'pompous' it is 'splendid; magnificent; grand', and then *The Deserted Village*, published fifteen years later.

> But the long pomp, the midnight masquerade,
> With all the freaks of wanton wealth arrayed,
> In these, ere triflers half their wish obtain,
> The toiling pleasure sickens into pain ...
> Here while the proud their long-drawn pomps display,
> There the black gibbet glooms beside the way ...

Pomp and pompous behaviour are now expressive of social irresponsibility. Those who are identified with 'pomp' – the splendour of wealth – use their money in ostentatious display. They are wholly indifferent to those to whom their forebears felt themselves beholden and for whose welfare they held themselves responsible. Jonson had extolled Penshurst because its walls were 'reared with no man's ruin, no man's groan'. It was not, he says, 'built to envious show'. It wasn't intended to over-awe. It might be a building of some pomp but it hadn't been built to over-awe or to form a self-congratulatory image of power and wealth.

During the eighteenth century a large number of country houses were built, especially by bankers and others of the newly rich. Such houses were pompous in Johnson's sense of the word: but they were also pompous in that newer sense Goldsmith drew on, one the *Oxford English Dictionary* defines as 'marked by an exaggerated display of self-importance or dignity; pretentious.' A glance at Blenheim Palace, presented to the Duke of Marlborough, after his victory at the Battle of Blenheim (1704) is enough to tell you why 'pomp' and 'pompous' necessarily shifted meaning or at least *nuance* in the eighteenth century. Villages, rural communities, were laid waste in order to improve the views from great houses, small farmers and labourers were thrown off the land as it was enclosed. The black gibbet was on public display as warning to those who dared oppose the new Laws of Privacy, of Poaching, of Land Ownership.

This and related matter is explored in Raymond Williams' *The Country and the City* and my own *England and Englishness: Poetry and National Identity 1688-1900*, but here it is enough to say that when Crabbe came to write the section of *The Parish Register* quoted above, he would have had Goldsmith as much in mind as he would Jonson. And he would certainly have been mindful of the fourth of Pope's Moral Essays on 'The Use of Riches', written in the early 1730s, which sets up the country house ideal as attainable but for the most part neglected by the pompous. Dedicated to Richard Boyle, Earl of Burlington, the poem praises the noble lord by claiming that 'You show us Rome was glorious, not profuse,/And pompous buildings once were things of use.'

Pope is here thinking of Burlington's town house, built on neo-classical lines, and supposedly an essential part of its surroundings in Piccadilly. Burlington also owned country estates, and Pope contrasts Burlington's care for these with the vanity of those who build and whose vast country houses often bring financial ruin and are themselves often destroyed, abandoned, pulled down, left as a pile of stones. The consideration of such ruins prompts some of Pope's greatest lines:

> Another age shall see the golden ear
> Embrown the slope and nod on the parterre;
> Deep harvests bury all his pride had planned,
> And laughing Ceres re-assume the land.

These lines envisage a return to benign nature. The Roman goddess of harvest, Ceres, will restore health to the land after the man of pompous wealth has sunk into a forgotten grave.

But the essential benignity of this vision, while it may be behind Crabbe's lines on the Lady of the Hall, isn't one that he chooses to sustain. Like Goldsmith, Crabbe's attention is concentrated on the ruinous consequences of the abandonment of responsibility by landowners, especially those who no longer 'dwell' in the houses of which they are the custodians. Jonson had ended 'To Penshurst' with these four lines:

> Now, Penshurst, they that will proportion thee
> With other edifices, when they shall see
> Those proud, ambitious heaps, and nothing else,
> May say, their lords have built, but thy lord dwells.

To 'dwell' is not merely to live in a particular place but to have your occupation there, to be committed to the place, morally and socially. King James had ordered owners of large houses to stay on the land, an order widely assumed to be not so much in the interests of keeping them loyal to their estates as to prevent them from forming possible cabals against the throne. This never became a legal requirement but in the following centuries the quasi-edict became a sort of moral imperative: dwelling was an integral part of the cement intended to bind different levels of society together in an ideal commonwealth.

Crabbe's Lady doesn't, however, dwell at the hall. She spends her time in town and entrusts the running of house and land to her 'Steward'. A steward, Johnson says, 'is one who manages the affairs of another'. And very interestingly, he quotes Swift: 'When a steward defrauds his lord, he must connive at the rest of the servants while they are following the same practice.' Stewards were often called 'faithful' by their employers, but the term implies a scarcely hidden anxiety. Suppose they weren't faithful at all? One of the emergent features of English social life during the eighteenth century was the degree to which owners of estates liked to put a distance between themselves and care of the land they owned. Not living above the shop – that desideratum of successful tradesmen in the nineteenth century – is anticipated in the social arrangements of landed gentry of an earlier age. It was stewards, or, as they were increasingly called, *managers*, who were entrusted with the day-to-day running of the estate. The owners wanted to have no observable part in the grubbiness of actual stewardship. Sometimes this posture of aloof ignorance was metaphorical, of not knowing what went on below stairs. More often it was actual. Town houses glittered with Society; country houses were associated with the dull routines of rural life.

But suppose while you were busy enjoying yourself in town, your steward or manager was getting ideas above his station?

Suppose he saw himself not merely as your deputy but as someone who could bring ruin on you by cheating on your estate, by cheating you *out* of your estate? During the eighteenth century, as has already been noted, a considerable number of landed estates fell into financial ruin, and although these were by no means always because of the crooked ways of stewards – the gambling habits of eldest sons were more often to blame – a kind of paranoia attached itself to the manner in which those who managed an estate's affairs were regarded. This would later be transferred to the uncertain fortunes of city businesses. Dickens' *Dombey and Son* (1848) features a man whose fortune is lost because of the way he is duped by his manager, Mr Carker. Dombey is too grand to get his fingers grubby with money matters. Those are left to Carker. He does all the dirty work. He also does for Dombey. And he does for others, too. He is a suave crook, a bully, someone who enjoys immiserating those dependent on the business he manages.

The steward who serves Crabbe's Lady is Carker's forebear. By upping the rents – and no doubt pocketing as much as he can of what the tenants have to pay him – he milks them of the little money they have; and he makes sure their complaints never reach the Lady's ears: 'The feeling servant spared the feeble dame.' As a result, she has no understanding of the ruination of her estate. 'She came not down her falling groves to view;/Why should she know what one so faithful knew?' Crabbe's sardonic wit, his uncomfortable mind, is here directed as much at the Lady as at the Steward. She brings ruin on herself and her death is made to feel ominously like the death, or at all events, decay of a way of life for long centuries associated with a responsible mutual relationship between master and men. In this, by the way, Crabbe not only anticipates *Dombey and Son* but Dickens' account in *Bleak House* (1853) of the Dedlock estate in Lincolnshire, melancholy, damp, decadent, with 'a general smell and taste as of the ancient

Dedlocks in their graves.'

Crabbe isn't as great as Dickens – no-one is – but he shares something of the imaginative intensity with which Dickens registers the mouldering decay of the Dedlock's 'place' in Lincolnshire, and with it the meaning of their place in English life, in the way he describes the interior of the Lady's house. 'No fire the kitchen's cheerless grate display'd'. Here is no hospitality. The household gods have departed. In its empty squalor the Hall has been invaded by 'The crawling worm that turns a summer fly' and which 'Here span his shroud and laid him up to die/The winter death.' Caterpillar to butterfly or conceivably moth to caddis: a grotesque parody of human occupation, from birth to death, stretched out by the run-on line. The sense seems complete with the word 'die', but the phrase 'the winter death' adds a shuddery frisson, one increased by the even more grotesque parody of sexuality played out by the bat 'upon the bed of state' which 'shrill shrieking woo'd his flickering mate.' Merely to speak that phrase 'shrill shrieking', which you have to take slowly, is to register what a master of saturnine comedy Crabbe is.

III

The Parish Register also shows Crabbe to be a master of what might be called social types, men and women alike. But ones who are never reduced to mere ciphers. His depiction in Part One of Phoebe Dawson, the seduced and abandoned village beauty, has a pathos which was rightly commented on by reviewers as both moving and original. Crabbe does not so much moralise Phoebe's 'fall' as grieve for it. Her story may be something of a set-piece but it is handled with a kind of discreet awareness of circumstance which, despite the admonishment of the couplet closing the tale off – 'Then fly temptation, youth; resist, refrain!/Nor let me preach for ever and in vain!' – has about it a real tenderness of regard, and while it is in the line of lonely outcasts that can be found in *The Deserted Village* and William Cowper's *The Task*, also has a particularity which marks it as Crabbe's own. The very fact that 'Phoebe' (an archetypal name for a country girl) is yoked to 'Dawson', makes the girl very different from the almost generic treatment of women outcasts to be found in the unnamed 'solitary thing' of Goldsmith's poem or Cowper's Crazy Kate. 'Dawson' is in fact a name associated with gypsies, though whether Crabbe intended to make the connection I doubt, given that elsewhere in his work gypsies are given short shrift; they are lawless, petty thieves, and dissolute. But at the very least Phoebe Dawson's name grounds her in actual rural circumstance.

And there is another point. The tripartite division of *The Parish Register* into 'Baptisms', 'Marriages' and 'Burials' makes possible a kind of conspectus of English provincial life that is unique in the poetry of its age, and, for that matter, in literature as a whole. At about the same time that Crabbe's first major poem was published, the Panorama would establish itself as a visual experience to which people flocked. In fact the first Panorama, an inclusive view of Edinburgh, was presented in that city in 1788, and in the early years of the nineteenth century London had several venues showing panoramas of the capital city and of sea-fights and land battles of the Napoleonic wars.

It would be inaccurate as well as misleading to describe *The Parish Register* as a panoramic poem. The focus is, after all, on scenes from provincial life rather than cities or events of national importance. In this it can perhaps be compared to the 'genre' paintings of the period made by Opie, Wilkie, Mulready, and their like, whose typical subject-matter included village events very similar to those about which Crabbe writes: births, marriages, funerals, the village pub, hunt meetings, and so on. *Ut pictura poesis* was a motto much appealed to during the eighteenth century. But there is a crucial difference between most genre painting and Crabbe, and it isn't merely that as a poet his scenes follow on from another whereas paintings are static depictions. They may depict movement but they exist in space rather than time. (It is true that Hogarth's sequences, *Marriage-à-la-Mode*, *The Rake's Progress*, etc create a narrative by showing us different, developing stages in a life, but inevitably each stage is itself 'fixed'.)

More importantly, most genre paintings take an essentially nostalgic and sometimes sentimental view of their subject matter. 'Go look within,' Crabbe had commanded in *The Village* of those who liked to depict thatched cottages, whether in word or paint, as places of tranquil contentment and modest sufficiency. *The Parish Register* looks within not merely at cottages but at grander houses and it does so with a critical, unsparing gaze. It was this which led to the enthusiastic reviews with which the poem was widely greeted. As the unsigned reviewer in the *Anti-Jacobin Review and Magazine* said, 'He may most truly be called the poet of nature who best delineates natural characters and natural scenes; and certainly no one displays more skill, in this kind of delineation, than Mr Crabbe. All his scenes, and all his characters, are, indeed, taken from common life, and chiefly from rural life.' Or in Jeffrey's words, in *The Edinburgh Review*, 'Mr Crabbe exhibits the common people of England pretty much as they are, and as they must appear to every one who will take the trouble of examining into their condition.'

Crabbe the realist deserves all the praise *The Parish Register* brought him, and it brought him a great deal. Three years later, perhaps buoyed by the critical and commercial success of his 1807 *Poems*, he seemingly returned to familiar ground, studies of rural life, when he published *The Borough*. But looking within now means something more. *The Parish Register* is the work of a genuinely original, important poet. With *The Borough* Crabbe becomes a great one.

4

The Borough (1810)

I

Reading the critical accounts of Crabbe's new poem prompts a number of reflections. The first is that those writing about *The Borough* take for granted that the author is a substantial poet. His work therefore merits detailed consideration. The second is that for the most part the critics not only welcome the poem, they write about it at length. And by length I mean anything from two to ten thousand words. The third is that the level of commentary is high. Crabbe could count himself fortunate to have been the object of so much intelligent, perceptive, sympathetic critical writing.

Not all of it was unambiguously celebratory. Several critics pointed to elements within *The Borough* of which they disapproved or about which they felt dubious. Crabbe was occasionally rapped over the knuckles for faults of construction, for poor rhymes, for an almost convulsive tic of verbal repetition, and sometimes for his at best pawky sense of humour and – very English, this – love of punning. The reviewer in *The Monthly Review* noted the desperate rhyme of the following couplet in Letter XII, 'Distress and hope – the mind's, the body's wear,/The man's affliction, and the actor's tear', a rhyme that works for the eye but not for the ear. But this is surely nit-picking. Eye rhymes are an accepted part of English poetry. Even Pope, perhaps the most resourceful of all rhymers, occasionally uses them. English is of all languages perhaps the most difficult to rhyme in, especially as it is a largely monosyllabic language. Peter Porter, himself a formidably gifted poet-as-rhymer, noted of Leslie Stephen's sneer at Crabbe's readiness to rhyme 'boy' with 'hoy' (a fishing vessel), that 'if Stephen had tried rhyming in English he'd have had more sympathy with Crabbe.' Agreed.

The *Monthly Review* was rather more justifiably sniffy about the punning couplet of Letter VI where Crabbe has 'Lest some attorney (pardon the poor name)/Should wound a poor solicitor of fame.' In an essay-length account of *The Borough* in *The Edinburgh Review*, Francis Jeffrey, perhaps Crabbe's most attentive critic, made plain his displeasure at such lines as 'We term it free and easy: and yet we/Find it no easy matter to be free' – too much of a jingle, that, Jeffrey complains; and as for 'Has your wife's brother, or your uncle's son,/Done aught amiss; or is he thought t'have done?', it is one example among several of what Jeffrey calls 'sudden, harsh turns, and broken conciseness.'

On the other hand, Jeffrey is alert to a style which he rightly identifies as 'distinguished, like all Mr Crabbe's other performances, by great force and compression of fiction, – a sort of sententious brevity.' And although a different critic perceptively called Crabbe 'the Hogarth of Poetry', it was Jeffrey who most memorably evoked Crabbe's ability to lead us, not 'through blooming groves and pastoral meadows', but 'along filthy lanes and crowded wharfs, to hospitals, alms-houses, and gin-shops. In some of these delineations,' Jeffrey adds, 'he may be considered the satirist of low life'; but his greater achievement is his success in 'moving or delighting us by lively, touching, and finely contrasted representations of the dispositions, sufferings, and occupations of those ordinary persons who form the greater part of our fellow-creatures.' And a little later, by way of adding to the soundness of this judgement, Jeffrey remarks that 'The familiar feeling of maternal tenderness and anxiety, which is every day before our eyes, even in the brute creation, – and the enchantment of youthful love, which is nearly the same in all characters, ranks and situations, – still contribute more to the beauty and interest of poetry than all the misfortunes of princes, the jealousies of heroes, and the feats of giants, magicians, and ladies in armour.'

Ladies in armour. This is Jeffrey's swipe at Southey, friend of Wordsworth and Coleridge, one of the 'Lake Poets', a writer Jeffrey intensely disliked, whose long dramatic poem, Joan of Arc, composed when Southey was still waving his radical colours, had appeared in the last years of the previous century. As for Jeffrey's fingering the appearances in contemporary poetry of unfortunate princes and jealous heroes, I suspect he will have had in mind his fellow countryman, Walter Scott, then known as a poet, his *Lay of the Last Minstrel* (1805) and *Marmion* (1808) having brought him both fame and fortune, as did *The Lady of the Lake*, which appeared in the same year as *The Borough*.

Scott's book-length poems are all by way of being narrative romances. Crabbe certainly knew and liked them, as he did their author, and it is even possible that the novels he wrote and burnt were similar in both theme and style to Scott's tales. But as Jeffrey's discriminative praise makes evident, *The Borough* is very different. Most readers, Jeffrey says, know little about princes, warriors, and banditti: 'but every one thoroughly understands every thing about cottages, streets, and villages; and conceives, pretty correctly, the character and condition of sailors, ploughmen and artificers ... It is human nature, and human feelings, after all, that form the true source of poetry in poetry of every description ... And [these] may be found as abundantly in the breasts of cottagers as of kings.' This is not only well said, it gets to the heart of much that is to be found in Crabbe's work.

True, some commentators thought the poet liable to overdo the kind of ordinariness Jeffrey praised him for attending to. In an unsigned review, Robert Grant in the *Quarterly Review*, the journal which was the *Edinburgh Review*'s great rival, rebuked Crabbe for his 'habit of automatically tracing and recording the deformities of his fellow-creatures', and for showing 'more of contempt than of tenderness' towards his characters, who, while they may be 'objects of his compassion are at the same time the objects of his satire.' But putting it rather differently, Grant acknowledges that Crabbe evinces 'little relish for the sentimental.' This is not only true, it is the product of what Forster unforgettably called Crabbe's 'uncomfortable mind'.

Add all these comments together and what emerges is an account of a writer who, if we didn't know differently, we would surely assume was a novelist in that great English tradition of social realism which, truth to tell, he does in many ways inaugurate. This is why so many nineteenth-century novelists admired Crabbe and learnt from him. When A.H. Clough, Matthew Arnold's friend, a very fine and disgracefully neglected poet, was pondering the difference between poetry and prose fiction in the middle years of the century, he said that novels 'do give us a real house to be lived in.' He meant that they were substantial in a way poems no longer seemed to be, dealt in the bricky particularities of social living. Clough himself wrote two novels in verse, part commentaries and part satires on aspects of mid-nineteenth-century life. The first, *The Bothie of Tober-na-Vuolich* (1848), about a group of Oxford students on a reading holiday in Scotland and the developing love affair between one of them and a local girl, ends with the couple's setting out for a new life together; the second, *Amours de Voyage* (first published in 1858 though written much earlier in the decade), is without much doubt a great piece of writing concerned with the English in Rome at the time of the *Risorgimento*. Neither owes much, if anything, directly to Crabbe, but both are made possible by the very fact that Crabbe brought into poetry lengthy tales of contemporary living.

Looking at what Jeffrey, that great admirer of Dickens, said of Crabbe, and taking especial note of his praise for the poet's sympathetic depiction of 'our fellow-creatures', it is, I think, inevitable that we recall some words of George Eliot, in the famous credo which occurs in chapter 17 of *Adam Bede*. 'These fellow-mortals, every one, must be accepted as they are,' she says; 'you can neither straighten their noses nor brighten their wit, nor rectify their dispositions; and it is these people – amongst whom your life is passed – that it is needful you should tolerate, pity, and love: it is these more or less ugly, stupid, inconsistent people, whose movements of goodness you should be able to admire – for whom you should cherish all possible hopes, all possible patience.' This is very close in many respects to Jeffrey's encomium about Crabbe.

But there is a difference. Grant's unease at the poet's readiness to 'indulge in a caustic raillery which may be mistaken for ill-nature', reminds us that the linking of Crabbe with Hogarth has its justification. Crabbe was not a man of feeling in the sense in which that phrase became used at the end of the eighteenth century, to identify and laud an expressive emotionalism as evidence of moral worth, which is what Grant seems to be recommending. Crabbe belongs to an older, harder, reasonableness, one Jane Austen shared. For her, a display of sensibility was too often taken by its champions as vindication without regard to consequence. 'Ah, what could we do but what we did,' as one of her early fictional yet-to-be-made-reasonable heroines tells a friend, 'We sighed and fainted on the sofa.' For Parson Crabbe, what you were was what you did: faith was in works.

Not only that. The unsentimental poet, well aware that peace was unlikely to be found in a cottage inhabited by destitute labourers, was also the poet who knew, as Dickens did and George Eliot did not, that evil, both as noun and verb, was real. It was how some people chose to be because it was what they chose to do. George Eliot especially cherished the art of the seventeenth-century Dutch masters who dealt in domestic interiors, ones which, in her words, 'provide faithful pictures of a monotonous homely existence ... an old woman bending over her flower-pot, or eating her solitary dinner ... the village wedding, kept between four brown walls, where an awkward bridegroom opens the dance with a high-shouldered, broad-faced wife, while elderly and middle-aged friends look on, with very irregular noses and lips, and probably with quart-pots in their hands ... ' Her art belongs to, and celebrates, a more meliorist view of human nature than Crabbe's.

II

As the poems by Clough mentioned above suggest, the novel in verse came to be a preoccupation with a number of nineteenth-century poets, including the greatest, Browning and Tennyson. Though *The Borough* is in some ways the precursor of such novels, it is more by way of being sketches, though so well marshalled that you feel it anticipates, if not the looser, wilder, more exuberant *Sketches by Boz*, then certainly such prose works as John Galt's *The Annals of the Parish* (1820 – the parish was a Lowlands Scottish one), and Mary Russell Mitford's *Our Village*, subtitled *Sketches of Rural Life, Character and Scenery*, which began life as a series of contributions to *The Lady's Magazine* in 1819, before appearing as five volumes between 1824-1832. The Berkshire village on which Mitford's sketches are based is, of course, very different from Crabbe's Borough: gentler, more whimsical, more – well, more lady-like, more like Elizabeth Gaskell's *Cranford* is usually and misleadingly reckoned to be.

This difference isn't merely one of place nor even of the author's gender. Many years ago, D.W. Harding famously identified 'regulated hatred' as a key element in Jane Austen's fiction. The difference I have in mind has most to do with the quality in Crabbe which Byron identified when he called him nature's 'sternest' painter, and he wasn't thinking merely of Crabbe's descriptions of the sea and land around Aldeburgh. Johnson defines 'stern' in character as 'Severe of manners; harsh; unrelenting; cruel', and he quotes as evidence the remark made by Coriolanus to his mother: 'My sometime general/I've seen thee stern, and thou has oft beheld/Heart hardening spectacles.' (Act IV, scene 1 – Johnson gives 'observed' for 'beheld').

Cruelty in Crabbe's poetry isn't a quality in the poet himself so much as of some of those about whom he writes, pre-eminently, though not exclusively, Peter Grimes; but his refusal to turn away from such cruelty is undoubtedly stern and this runs throughout the twenty-four 'Letters' that make up *The Borough*. These letters are supposedly being written for someone living in a very different setting from the sea-side town from which the correspondent himself writes. During the eighteenth century, the publication of Letters became something of a vogue. Among the more famous of such publications are Samuel Richardson's epistolary novels *Pamela* and *Clarissa*, and the scarcely less famous Letters in which the Earl of Chesterfield instructed his son how to live as a true gentleman; but, Richardson aside, the most popular such publication was Gilbert White's *The Natural History and Antiquities of Selborne in the County of Southampton*. This was first published in 1789, a second, revised and expanded edition appeared in 1802, and since then it has never been out of print.

Like Crabbe, White was in holy orders, and also like him, he was a keen naturalist. To judge from publications alone, so frequent is this conjunction among the Anglican clergy of the period between 1750-1900, that it's possible to feel the Church of England's main function was to give employment to natural historians. Certainly, Crabbe used his opening Letter to footnote references to the large Lily ('the white water-lily, Nymphaea alba' and 'Samphire-banks[+] and [++] Saltwort' ('[+] the jointed glasswort. Salicornia, is here meant, not the true samphire, the Crithmum maritime' '[++]The Salsola of botanists').

Further footnotes depart from the observations of the natural historian to suggest that the letter-writer is a gentleman of curious observation of the minutiae of daily living. Of the curvature of planks for boats, the writer tells his correspondent that it is, 'I am informed, now generally made by the power of steam. Fire is nevertheless still used for boats and vessels of the smaller kind', and that the property of fog-banks 'of appearing to elevate ships at sea, and to bring them in view, is, I believe, generally acknowledged.'

White's Letters were addressed to an actual correspondent, 'Thomas Pennant, Esquire'. Crabbe's is pure fiction but he cleverly imagines the recipient of the letters to be an upland dweller, something of a hermit. Can the scenes the writer sets out to describe, he wonders:

> withdraw thee from thy wood,
> Thy upland forest, or thy valley's flood?
> Seek then thy garden's shrubby bound, and look,
> As it steals by, upon the bordering brook;
> That winding streamlet, limpid, lingering, slow,
> Where the reeds whisper when the zephyrs blow ...
> Draw then the strongest contrast to that stream,
> And our broad river will before thee seem.

And so, having invented a correspondent who will know nothing of a bustling sea-side town, the writer licenses himself to supply in Twenty-Four Letters the features of the Borough: its institutions, its amusements, its professions, its businesses, and, above all, its citizens. As to who the writer actually is, it seems safe to say that, if not Crabbe himself, he is sufficiently like the poet for us to regard him as a reliable narrator. We see through his eyes, and we aren't intended to speculate on the possible distortions of his vision. The person who writes the Letters which make up *The Borough* means to be a truthful interpreter of all that he sees. And he sees a great deal. Because there's very little point in differentiating between the Letter-writer and poet, I intend to call him Crabbe in the following pages.

III

Letters Two, Three, and Four of *The Borough* are about the church and religious matters. This is unsurprising, although it takes some effort in our largely post-Christian age to realise the high degree to which religion, especially Anglicanism, dominated village and town at the time Crabbe was writing, a dominance that continued, with gradually lessening strength, until far into the twentieth century. The church was at the centre of social and cultural life. Its norms were society's norms. Baptisms, marriages, and burials, happened within its doors. It stood for what seemed to be intrinsic English values. Anglicanism was inevitably monarchical (it came into existence through the needs of Henry VIII), hierarchical, and sceptical of too much pomp, let alone piety. The former was for Catholics, the latter for non-Conformists. As Lord Melbourne, Victoria's favourite prime minister, once muttered, 'Prayer in private is going a damned sight too far.'

It also needs to be remembered that the church was *visibly* an important feature of English life. Churches, many of them built while England was a Catholic nation, though this was not a matter much adverted to, habitually stood on high ground, their steeples, or, more rarely, towers, aspiring to heaven. Around each church was God's acre, that stretch of green ground where, in Thomas Gray's famous phrase, 'The rude forefathers' of the town, village, or hamlet, lay. (The marble tombs of the local gentry and lords and ladies were inside the church, inviting respectful awareness as you sang and prayed.) Nearby, the vicarage, usually a large, imposing building, reinforced the church's standing and the vicar's central role in the community's affairs.

Letter Two of *The Borough* opens with the question, 'What is a Church?' The answer is, that if not all things to all men, the Church means different things to different men. To the vicar, it is a 'a flock ... whom bishops govern and whom priests advise'; to the sexton the church is 'a tall building with a tower and bells'; and to others it is a place they go to worship, to see and be seen. Crabbe doesn't spend much time on any of these matters. He is more interested in describing the church's fabric and interior, which he does in a manner of which John Betjeman would, you feel, approve, though as far as I know Betjeman has nothing to say about Crabbe. But how well, how sardonically, Crabbe describes what he calls 'a tomb of grandeur':

> That marble arch, our sexton's favourite show,
> With all those ruff'd and painted pairs below;
> The noble Lady and the Lord who rest
> Supine, as courtly dame and warrior drest;
> All are departed from their state sublime,
> Mangled and wounded in their war with Time
> Colleagued with mischief; here a leg is fled,
> And lo! the Baron with but half a head;
> Midway is cleft the arch; the very base
> Is batter'd round and shifted from its place.

Never mind Betjeman. No wonder Hardy so admired Crabbe, sharing as he does that laconic, dark humour which undoes the claims of entitlement to enduring dignity. 'Ah, Are you digging on my grave?' the underground speaker of one Hardy poem is imagined asking her faithful dog – to which the dog replies

> 'Mistress, I dug upon your grave
>   To bury a bone, in case
> I should be hungry near this spot
> When passing on my daily trot.
> I am sorry, but I quite forgot
>   It was your resting place.'

'Here a leg is fled/And lo! the Baron with but half a head.' And Time, that reverend sire, is here 'Colleagued with mischief', the line-break exactly poised to undo grandeur.

Crabbe ends the Letter with the sad story of a very ordinary couple, their courtship prolonged by the young man's life as a sailor intent on wanderings which eventually bring him home to die. Vicar Crabbe will not accord more space to the Baron and his Dame than to this couple, though he speaks up for Sense in chiding the woman's prolonged grief. It may be genuine but it isn't reasonable. 'Thy patient spirit to thy duties give,/Regard the dead, but to the living live.' But the writer adds an anxious footnote to the closing phrase, in which he explains that he means to imply that the woman should 'attend to duties only which are real, and not those imposed by the imagination.' Reading that, it is impossible not to recall the moment near the end of *Sense and Sensibility* where Elinor Dashwood replies to her sister's near-incredulous question about how she managed to sustain herself in the face of near-heartbreak by saying that she felt it her duty to do so. No wonder Jane Austen felt herself so in sympathy with Crabbe.

She would also have found much to admire in the accounts of vicar and curate that fill out the next two Letters. The vicar in particular, though not a rival to the insufferable Mr Collins of *Pride and Prejudice*, is, as is well noted in the extended report on *The Borough* in the *Critical Review*, 'free from vice, because he is exempt from passion and feeling, who acts not wrong because he has not energy to act at all … whose virtue is without worth because it is without effort; whose benevolence evaporates in words; whose life is mere vegetation.' The vicar's constant care, Crabbe tells us, 'was no man to offend'. This runs the risk of making him seem a kind of Pecksniffian humbug; but with great dexterity Crabbe makes the vicar a more interesting case of enervate good-will, and in so doing signals the start of something new in his work: a psychological acuity which provides yet another cause of his being so intensely admired by nineteenth-century novelists. This acuity is also, I think, new to English poetry.

> Mild were his doctrines, and not one discourse
> But gain'd in softness what it lost in force:
> Kind his opinions; he would not receive
> An ill report, nor evil act believe;
> 'If true, 'twas wrong; but blemish great or small
> Have all mankind; yea, sinners are we all.'

Augustan poetry, we are used to being told, thrives on balance, the give and take of thesis and antithesis. These lines are a perfect example of such balance, but what gives them their comic distinction is Crabbe's ability, sardonic and yet deftly poised, to allow sympathy to a man whose tepidity, as much emotional as moral, defeats criticism. Of course, as a Christian the vicar *should* believe in the possibility of evil acts; but as a man who instinctively wants to swerve from the responsibility of condemning sin, he can, without self-accusation, appeal to the truth that we are all sinners. To call the vicar bland is to miss the point. He is an altogether trickier being: someone who resists *any* classification.

The curate, on the other hand, is a man of religion but also of crippling poverty, as such men often were. Vicars could afford to spend months away from their parishes – Crabbe himself had done so – but they still received their stipends, though in the early years of the nineteenth century the church began to toughen up on absentee incumbents. Curates, however, were famously 'poor as church mice'. They might well be younger sons of gentlemen, offloaded onto the church because there was no other way for their father to provide for them. Of course they hoped for modest advancement to a vicarage; but as preferment was typically in the hands of those who would give the nod to sons of friends and family, curates could die as poor as they had lived.

So it is with Crabbe's curate. A man of genuine piety and learning, he would, Crabbe says, have done better for himself had he been 'apprenticed to a humble trade,/Had he the cassock for the priesthood made,/Or thrown the shuttle, or the saddle shaped,/And all those pangs of feeling souls escaped'. Instead, he is forced to live in penury with his wife 'Where he from view, though not from want retires;/Where four fair daughters, and five sorrowing sons,/Partake his sufferings and dismiss his duns'.

> Some Tradesman's bill his wandering eyes engage,
> Some scrawl for payment thrust 'twixt page and page;
> Some bold, loud rapping at his humble door,
> Some surly message he has heard before,
> Awake alarm, and tell him he is poor.
> An angry dealer, vulgar, rich, and proud,
> Thinks of his bill and, passing, raps aloud;
> The elder daughter meekly makes him way –
> 'I want my money and I cannot stay:
> My mill is stopp'd; what, Miss! I cannot grind;
> Go tell your father he must raise the wind.'

Johnson would not have approved Crabbe's use of the colloquialism about raising the wind, nor will you find such salty exactness in Wordsworth, who, for all his talk about using the real language of men, was quick to explain in the famous Preface to the *Lyrical Ballads* that he had taken care to ensure such language was 'purified indeed from what appeared to be its real defects' before allowing it into his poems.

To this we must add another matter of some significance. Crabbe's depiction of the poor curate, forced to endure 'rude and fierce attacks' and 'the want of bread', introduces to English poetry a kind of existence that would become increasingly common, or at all events increasingly remarked, as the nineteenth century wore on. The curate is an example, one of the first in English poetry, of the phenomenon that came to be known as shabby-gentility.

As far as I am aware it was Dickens who coined the phrase shabby-genteel. In one of the finest of his *Sketches by Boz*, he describes a down-at-heels city-dweller who 'feels his poverty and vainly strives to conceal it' and who is 'one of the most pitiable objects in human nature. Such objects, with few exceptions, are shabby-genteel people.' Dickens being Dickens he makes a most powerful, haunting sketch out of them. But it was Crabbe who brought such people into English literature.

IV

Crabbe prefaces the fourth Letter with a lengthy prose Apologia. He obviously felt the need to justify himself from what he feared might be a disapproval of his treatment of Dissent, a disapproval he labels 'the violence of causeless resentment'; and to head this off, he explains that what he calls 'Enthusiastical teachers', by whom he means Calvinist and Armenian Methodists, often work on 'weak minds' by means of bigotry, folly and craft. This is in the grand tradition of Anglican polemics and reminiscent of the lines in 'Religio Laici', where Dryden, having remarked that 'Points obscure are of small use to learn,/But common quiet is mankind's concern', lays into those who find in the bible justification for their own beliefs, no matter how bizarre or dangerous to the common quiet.

> This was the fruit the private spirit brought,
> Occasion'd by great zeal but little thought;
> The unlearn'd crowd, with rude devotion warm,
> About the sacred viands buzz and swarm,
> The fly-blown text creates a crawling brood,
> And turns to maggots what was meant for food.

Wonderful, visceral polemics, and unyielding in its hauteur: the 'unlearn'd' are, it first seems, to be complimented for their rude devotion; but then we realise that such 'warmth' turns the meat – the bible – maggoty rotten.

Crabbe can't match this tone of contempt, this magnificent, almost Coriolanus-like contempt for the private spirit. But he is certainly roused against what he considers to be preaching that is a danger not merely to people's peace of mind but the peace of the community.

> None of my readers will, I trust, do me so much injustice as to suppose that I have here any other motive than a vindication of what I have advanced in the verses which describe this kind of character [of Methodist preachers], or that I had any other purpose than to express (what I conceive to be) justifiable indignation against the assurance, the malignity, and (what is of more importance) the pernicious influence, of such sentiments on the minds of the simple and ignorant, who, if they give credit to his relations, must

be no more than tools and instruments under the control and management of one called to be their Apostle. (The square brackets are mine, the rounded brackets are Crabbe's.)

That's telling 'em.

To understand this uncharacteristic vehemence we need to realise that at the time Crabbe was writing, Dissent in the shape of not merely Methodism but of various millenarian and chiliastic sects (including Joanna Southcott's) were becoming deeply attractive to a growing number of people who saw themselves as excluded from the Anglican community. Dissent is, in other words, part of the story of the complicating of social relationships – of master and men, of class – that characterise the period 1780-1830. The zealots or Enthusiasts took inspiration from preachers – charismatic leaders and Apostles of a new order – whose fire-brand politics could not be separated from the events taking place in revolutionary France.

This, anyway, was the fear among those who preferred 'common quiet'. Crabbe never overtly acknowledges his own fear that the influence of the kind of Apostle he writes about in Letter IV may lead to civil disorder, but he hardly needed to because his readers would have understood his meaning. They would also have seen chapels of various denominations being constructed, mostly on the edges of towns and villages across the country, would have sensed in the construction of these how the powerful allure of the Anglican church was being literally displaced, and, were they to read Crabbe, would have good reason to be bewildered by, and fearful of, the various sects all of which insisted on the absolute truth of their own version of 'revealed' religion, whether that was Calvinistic (which took for granted predestination) or Arminian (preaching the opposite), or whether it proved to lie with other, more extreme or indeed bizarre interpretations of the Good

Book. As Crabbe puts it in a footnote to a passage where he describes one preacher telling his 'flock' that the story of Samson has to be interpreted to mean that the virtuous 'must in bondage groan', 'Whoever has attended to the books or preaching of these enthusiastic people, must have observed much of this kind of absurd and foolish application of Scripture history; it seems to them as reasoning.'

V

It may therefore be no accident that the following Letter, V, deals with 'The Election'. I doubt Crabbe intends a pun on the term, although certain sects did insist that they were of the 'Elect', meaning the specially chosen of God. But it is wittily apt that *The Borough* should move from the contentious brabble of religious sects to the brawls of secular politics. And Crabbe's account of pre-election shenanigans is, *mutatis mutandis*, certainly reminiscent of Hogarth's great depictions of an Election as the opportunity for drunken carnival, for mayhem, punch-ups, license.

> Yes, our election's past, and we've been free,
> Somewhat as madmen without keepers be;
> And such desire of Freedom has been shown,
> That both the parties wish'd her all their own:
> All our free smiths and cobblers in the town
> Were loth to lay such pleasant freedom down;
> To put the bludgeon and cockade aside,
> And let us pass unhurt and undefied.

This is how Letter V opens, and it continues in a similar caustic vein, one that, while it certainly recalls Hogarth, also anticipates Dickens' treatment of the Eatonswill Election in *The Pickwick*

Papers. Though only Dickens could have come up with 'Eatonswill' to characterise some of the shameless bribery in which the candidates indulged, where likely voters were seduced, as Crabbe has it in a brilliant line, by 'What fill'd their purses, and what drench'd their throats', and which inevitably led on election night to scenes of brutality as much as hilarity: fist-fights, spewings up, broken limbs and heads.

Crabbe ends the Letter by rather withdrawing from the rambunctious account of the election in order to suggest that, after all, it's in a good cause. However much the excesses are to be regretted, he says, 'These ill effects from noble cause proceed', because 'The tree they spring from is a sacred tree,/And its true produce, Strength and Liberty.' Throughout English history trees have symbolised the coming together of people in a political cause. Their sheltering branches suggest strength and protection, their size and deep-rootedness a kind of chthonic truth, one that embodies natural rights. Hence, Robin Hood's major oak, the Norfolk oak under which the men of Kett's rebellion in the middle years of the sixteenth-century gathered, the elm in Dorset under which in 1834 the six Tolpuddle martyrs met to insist on their rights as agricultural workers, the sycamore beneath which some thirty years later Joseph Arch stood in rural Warwickshire as he created the first Agricultural Workers' Union.

But in 1810 two trees in particular stood for 'Strength and Liberty'. One was the Liberty Tree associated with the French Revolution, the other, its opposite, the tree of State Edmund Burke appealed to when he argued that a nation grows by slow, natural process, and that to try to change it of a sudden – to make a 'root and branch' reform – would be tantamount to destroying it. Liberty trees were planted to celebrate a victory over oppression, or tyranny, or enemies of freedom. The frequently reproduced image of such a tree, newly planted, typically showed Phrygian caps in place of leaves. The 'caps' were conical bonnets with the top turned over in front and were much worn by French revolutionaries as symbols of their liberation.

For Burke, on the other hand, fearful of what he regarded as the lawless energies which the Revolution released, only the old, deep-rooted tree of a shared heritage could adequately symbolise a healthy state, and it is this which Crabbe has in mind when he speaks of the 'sacred tree/And its true produce, Strength and Liberty.' Crabbe, we must remember, owed a great debt to Burke, whose work *Reflections on the Revolution in France, and on the proceedings in certain societies in London relative to that event,* to give it its full title, he would certainly have read, either when it appeared in 1790, or soon after.

But the endorsement of Burke's tree of state is not merely a matter of form. Crabbe was a natural conservative, another reason for Jane Austen's intuitive sympathy with him. I don't think this makes him in any sense complacent about the society he found about him, but it does make him sceptical about claims for sudden change and distrustful of those who championed them. Crabbe is a Johnsonian Tory. Burke, it is true, was officially a Whig – defined by Johnson as 'a member of a faction' – but he shared Johnson's fear of anything that smacked of sedition or which threatened civil unrest. He was for moderation, though noting with approval Johnson's capacity for immoderate enjoyment when it came to food and drink, as well as relishing the oddities and quirks of human behaviour.

There will be more to say about Crabbe's writing about such oddities. But first a word or two on the Letters that follow on The Election. These deal with The Law (Letter VI), Physic (Letter VII), Trades (Letter VIII) and Amusements (Letter IX). All are of interest and the last of these, in particular, deserves attention if only because of the brilliantly-conducted narration of a boating party cut off by the advancing tide whose adventure nearly ends in disaster. If you want to know where

Jean Ingelow got the inspiration for her famous sob-story poem, 'High Tide on the Coast of Lincolnshire,1571', first published in 1863 and a best-seller for the remaining years of the century, look no further.

VI

Letter X concerns 'Clubs and Social Meetings' and here, as so often in *The Borough*, we can see something new happening, something that we might expect from the poet who was prepared to allow the idiomatic utterance about raising the wind, but which now, quite suddenly, becomes vital to his poetry. Crabbe peers in on a Smokers' Club. More importantly, he *listens* to the talk.

> 'Then, as I said, and – mind me – as I say,
> At our last meeting – you remember?' – 'Ay'
> 'Well, very well – then freely as I drink
> I spoke my thought – you take me – what I think.
> And, sir, said I, if I a freeman be,
> It is my bounden duty to be free'
> 'Ay, there you posed him; I respect the Chair,
> But man is man, although the man's a mayor;
> If Muggins live – no, no! – if Muggins die,
> He'll quit his office – neighbour, shall I try?'
> 'I'll speak my mind, for here are none but friends:
> They're all contending for their private ends;
> No public spirit – once a vote would bring,
> I say a vote – was then a pretty thing;
> It made a man to serve his country and his king:
> But for that place, that Muggins must resign,
> You've my advice – 'tis no affair of mine.'

Wonderful stuff. Two archetypal club bores, both the worse for drink, neither paying much attention to the other, but full of absurd gravitas, of bombast, huffed up with dignity and clichés which they offer each other as profound truths. All at once, Crabbe has become a comic writer.

This dialogue points the way to some of the effects Crabbe takes further in *Tales in Verse*, although oddly he forswears it in Letter XI, where you might well expect to find it, given that the Letter in question is about Inns. The main interest of this Letter is, in fact, in the various types of hostelry Crabbe covers: from what he calls 'the principal inn and those of the first class' down to 'a lower kind of Public-Houses … Houses of the Quays for Sailors – The Green Man; its Landlord, and the Adventure of his Marriage, etc'. Like most of the Letters, XI includes an anecdote about a character or characters who are identified with the life and/or occupation the different Letters detail, though I have to say that the story about the Innkeeper and his conversion from roisterer to marriage and fatherhood is something of a plod.

Not so the following Letter XII, which is about Players. The Borough is visited by a travelling troupe, which although not in the Crummles class or likely to outdo Mr Wopsle as Hamlet, is nevertheless good value, not all of it comic. Some of it assuredly is, though, for the audience, which assembles to witness the fare the travellers serve up, is determined to have a good time:

> [For] then our servants' and our seamen's wives,
> Love all that rant and rapture as their lives:
> He who Squire Richard's part could well sustain,
> Finds as King Richard he must roar amain –
> 'My horse! My horse!' – Lo! now to their abodes,
> Come lords and lovers, empresses and gods …
> Long as our custom lasts they gladly stay,
> Then strike their tents, like Tartars! and away.

The place grows bare where they too long remain,
But grass wll rise ere they return again.

So these wandering, or as Crabbe calls them 'itinerant' players belong to the world of 'fit-up' theatre. The borough doesn't seem to have a purpose-built theatre. Crabbe has a footnote worrying that he may have been too harsh on the players, 'their profligacy exaggerated, and their distresses magnified.'

But the life of wandering players *was* hard. For evidence of this we need look no further than Hogarth's 'The Strolling Players, Dressing in a Barn' (as it became known, though the artist originally advertised the work by the more titillating title 'Strolling Actresses dressing in a Barn'.) A commentator on this work, prints of which reached the market in 1738, notes that 'such is the [actors'] poverty, that they have but one room for all purposes; witness the bed, the gridiron, the food, and all the stage apparatus; *viz.* scenes, flags, paint-pots, pageants, brushes, clouds, waves, ropes, besoms, drums, trumpets, salt-boxes, and other musical instruments; crowns, mitres, helmets, targets, dark lanterns, cushions, periwigs, feathers, hampers of jewels, and contrivances for conjuring, thunder, lightning, dragons, daggers, poison, candles, and clay.'

A hundred years after Hogarth's print went on sale, Dickens' *Nicholas Nickleby* depicts the life of a travelling company, the Crummles, in a manner which, following Hogarth and Crabbe, is genially comic but makes clear that to survive such a life required a good deal of grit. Crabbe not only shows us this, he also communicates the unembarrassed relish of the audience for the histrionic fare his travelling troupe dish up, from farce (Squire Richard) to Shakespearian tragedy. And as with so much else in *The Borough*, part of the fascination comes from the fact that Crabbe is so informative as well as entertaining – a social historian on non-metropolitan England. He tells you things you can't find anywhere else.

VII

The Letters on Alms-Houses, Prisoners and the Poor are of a piece with most of *The Borough*: alert, sympathetic, full of matter. They also contain studies of some individuals which, in their imaginative reach and psychological awareness, indubitably put Crabbe among the greatest of English poets. Before I come to these, though, I need to mention a passage in Letter XVIII. The lines I have especially in mind form a *tour-de-force* of detailed description of some of the flora Crabbe had studied, and they are full of the kind of detail which, while not unique to him, is rare enough to command a kind of awed admiration, as well as quizzical speculation as to the reasons he was drawn to plants that other botanist-poets, such as his contemporary, Erasmus Darwin, were inclined to pass by without comment.

True, Darwin's long poem, 'Loves of the Plants' (1789), part of his full-dress *Botanic Garden*, is an exercise in versifying Linnaean principles of classification as well as explaining the reproductive systems of plant-life (an enterprise in which he was so graphically successful that Ruskin was not alone among later commentators in exhorting parents to keep the work from the eyes of young women); but Darwin has little interest to those lowly, intrusive weeds which fascinate Crabbe in his wanderings through the Borough's back lanes, as he comes across shacks, shanties, tumble-down sheds and cottages, and sees

> There, fed by food they love, to rankest size,
> Around the dwellings docks and wormwood rise;
> Here the strong mallow strikes her slimy root,
> Here the dull nightshade hangs her deadly fruit:
> On hills of dust the henbane's faded green,
> And pencil'd flower of sickly scent is seen;
> At the wall's base the fiery nettle springs,

With fruit globose and fierce with poison'd stings;
Above (the growth of many a year) is spread
The yellow level of the stone-crop's bed:
In every chink delights the fern to grow,
With glossy leaf and tawny bloom below;
These, with our sea-weeds, rolling up and down,
Form the contracted Flora of the town.

Crabbe provides a characteristic footnote to the passage. 'The reader, unacquainted with the language of botany, is informed that the Flora of a place means the vegetable species it contains, and is the title of a book which describes them.' The inference we are entitled to draw from this is that, to all intents and purposes, *The Borough*, in itself, constitutes such a book. So it does, and it is worth noting that in later years, when Crabbe became friendly enough with Wordsworth for the two to take country walks together around Trowbridge, the Somerset town to which Crabbe moved as vicar in 1815, Wordsworth was amazed at the extent of his companion's knowledge of the lowliest plants and, in particular, of grasses. And though I would not defend every word of the above passage – Crabbe just about gets away with the tongue-in-cheek 'fruit globose', but not the awkwardly inverted syntax of the line about the fern – the fact remains that the lines are rich in detailed observation of a kind both unusual and indicative of the poet's pharmaceutical training. Apothecary Crabbe would have known that the henbane's flower produced juice that was both narcotic and poisonous. Hence, the laconic pun on 'sickly'. And countryman Crabbe would have been well aware that poor people often grew stone-crop on their walls in order to pick the leaves for spring salads.

It would be silly to argue that Crabbe's almost obsessive interest in these forms of plant life implies a kind of displaced consciousness of his own humble beginnings. But he certainly didn't shrink from acknowledging the way life is rooted in mud and muck. The food on which dock, wormwood and mallow thrive is made up of waste stuff thrown out by households and includes human excrement. 'Dust hill' was then and during later times the accepted term for what, in another such term, were the heapings left by the 'night-soil' men – garbage and refuse collectors, of those who carried off the emptied-out contents of earth closets. In *Our Mutual Friend*, the 'golden dustman', Mr Boffin, grows rich from raking through the dust heaps he gathers and finding in them discarded matter he can sell on. Money and muck go together.

But for certain of the Poor, who are the subjects of Letters XIX-XXII, money proves elusive. And it is in his studies of The Parish Clerk (XIX), Ellen Orford (XX), Abel Keene (XXI) and Peter Grimes (XXII) that Crabbe does something that was, to borrow Milton's proud boast about *Paradise Lost*, until then unattempted in prose or rhyme. Because what he does *is* so new, the sour comment of the anonymous commentator in the *Critical Review* is explicable if not sustainable: 'we cannot help mentioning,' the critic says, 'the author's very unpoetical habit of giving two names to his heroes and heroines … This frequently gives an air of drollery to the most pathetic passages, and is too familiar even for the most familiar narrative.' (CH, p.107) There is no explanation of why this should be so, but I assume that the critic looks for a certain archetypal element to 'poetic' characters. Country men and women ought to be called Colin or Phoebe, not Ellen Orford or Abel Keene or, of course, Phoebe Dawson.

Crabbe, however, knows exactly what he is doing. There is a resonance to these names, one that helps us to grasp something about their bearers. Orford was a small town near Aldeburgh, and by so naming the poor woman he writes about, Crabbe gives her a kind of rootedness, a belonging to the place where she lives. Abel Keene is a man eager to do well and who eventually falls into disgrace. Keen he may be, able he is not. Object to the name Crabbe gives him and you might as well object to Henry James' calling the would-be high-flying heroine of *The Portrait of a Lady* Isobel Archer, to take a random example of the way in which novelists have often gone about naming their characters.

Francis Jeffrey's objection to a character such as Keene is rather different. Much as Ruskin would later complain that the Spanish artist Murillo inspired no tender feelings for the poor because he insisted on depicting them warts and all, so, according to Jeffrey, Crabbe makes his readers 'turn away … with loathing and dispassionate aversion' from 'those festering heaps of moral filth and corruption.' Crabbe, he goes on, is unique in 'present[ing] us with spectacles which it is purely painful and degrading to contemplate, and bestow[ing] such powers of conception and expression in giving us distinct ideas of what we must abhor to remember.' (The passage is to be found in *Crabbe: The Critical Heritage*, ed. Arthur Pollard, p. 92. All future references to this work will be identified as CH). If Crabbe had been less good we could have better borne what he shows, seems to be the nub of Jeffrey's argument.

The Letter concerning Ellen Orford is exempt from these criticisms, which others, their stomachs no stronger than Jeffrey's, shared. All reviewers concur in their estimation of Crabbe's noteworthy success in writing in Letter XX about a woman whose Christian acceptance of the difficulties with which her life is beset. At the head of the poem Crabbe sets out what we are to encounter. 'Her employment in Childhood – First Love; first Adventure; its miserable termination. – An idiot Daughter – An Husband. – Care in Business without Success. – The Man's Despondency, and its Effect. – Their Children: how disposed of. – One particularly unfortunate. – Fate of the Daughter. – Ellen keeps a school and is happy. – Becomes blind: loses her School. Her Consolations.'

Reading this it is difficult not to think of Oscar Wilde on one of Dickens' early heroines. 'He must have a heart of stone who can read of the death of Little Nell without laughing.' But although Crabbe's own summary seems virtually a parodic account of misfortune and suffering, he manages the extraordinarily difficult feat of making Ellen Orford both credible and intensely sympathetic. This is partly because at the outset he does what Jane Austen does in *Northanger Abbey*: contrast the fantastic sufferings of the protagonists of Gothic romances with the sufferings of real flesh and blood. 'Time have I lent – I wish their debt was less – /To flower pages of sublime Distress,' the Letter begins, having first invited the reader of his Letter to observe a 'Tenement, apart and small,/Where the wet pebbles shine upon the wall.' Real suffering happens here, not in fancied chateaux or 'in Forest wide/And caverns vast.'

Crabbe's sharply funny and sardonic demolition of such romances takes up more than a hundred lines but is justified by what follows: his detailed account of a life that feels authentically sad but which is braced by a faith not to be mocked. 'I love mankind and call my God my friend.' That final line might seem ridiculous. What, after all you've gone through, you can still claim that? But, yes, she can. Resignation goes with a kind of obduracy that dispels our scepticism.

That it should do so depends very much on Crabbe's convincing us that Ellen *would* feel as she says she does. And he brings this off because instead of himself narrating her story he lets her tell it in her own words, which she does with a kind of calm, measured steadiness as psychologically convincing as it is deeply attractive. Ellen is a good woman, entirely without sanctimony or self-pity. James Montgomery, himself a poet of some distinction, calls her tale 'a signal example of patience under a complication of distress,' (CH, p.105), which is well said. 'Tragedy should be a great kick at misery,' Lawrence said, when repudiating Arnold Bennett's way of depicting characters to whom things happen without their answering back, as it were. But patience isn't quite the same as resignation, and the gap between them is the space Ellen Orford occupies. To make a memorable distinction Robert Frost insisted on: grief is not grievance or grievances, which Frost characterised as a 'form of impatience'. Instead, grief is 'a form of patience'. Ellen Orford does not nurse grievances.

Montgomery didn't think so well of Letter XXI. Nor did other reviewers. It's certainly an odd story. The Abel Keene who tells his life story is an old man remembering the follies that led to his abandoning the occupation of clerk in a counting-house in the hope of becoming, so Montgomery rather histrionically puts it, 'infidel, beau, and debauchee'. Keene is a shabby-genteel gentleman who in a timorous way aims for life as a Regency buck. Crabbe dextrously interweaves his own narrative account of Keene's life with the man's own words and with those of his sister, whose scorn for Abel's pretensions is prompted by remorseless good sense. 'What pains, my brother, dost thou take to prove/A taste for follies which thou canst not love?/Why do thy stiffening limbs the steed bestride/That lads may laugh to see thou canst not ride.'

The tale of Abel Keene ends, conventionally, we may feel, with Abel's words of contrition – 'Alas for me, no more the times of peace/Are mine on earth – in death my pains may cease' – even if the Letter's dark humour has an almost Swiftian feel to it. But what comes next is of a different order altogether.

VIII

Peter Grimes – to shorten the title of Letter XXII – is the one poem by which Crabbe is still widely known, though this is almost certainly because of Benjamin Britten's opera version.

But splendid though the incidental music for this is, it gives a misleading and sentimentalised account of the poem. Britten's Grimes is a man who, for all his brutality, is presented as a misunderstood outcast. The opera's gay sub-text requires the audience to feel pity for Grimes. Crabbe's great poem is altogether harder in its account of a man whose lapses into self-pity are typical of a brutal bully. The narrator's voice, shrewd, un-illusioned, sees through Grimes' occasional displays of maudlin emotion. His background isn't to be blamed for his nature. His mum and dad don't fuck him up.

Grimes' father is a hard-working fisherman, devout, civil, content with his laborious life, and intent on bringing up his son to share his own values.

> But soon the stubborn boy from care broke loose,
> At first refused, then added his abuse:
> His father's love he scorned, his power defied,
> But being drunk, wept sorely when he died.

Peter feels momentary shame at his scornful denunciation of his father's attempts to control his rebellious nature, but he is determined 'To prove his Freedom and assert the Man'. I give this line with the capitalised nouns as it was first printed, because they make plain Crabbe's implication that Peter is able to justify the desire to please himself by appealing, however cynically, to the language of a new politics – that of the Rights of Man. Thomas Paine's seminal work was first published in 1791 and immediately became one of the most celebrated works of its time, reviled by many, ardently championed by others. Paine himself, famously an atheist, died in exile in America in 1809, having previously spent time in revolutionary France, although he became an opponent of the revolution's increasingly bloody methods and in 1794 was imprisoned there for eleven months. His return to America in 1802 was not without controversy, despite his championing of Independence, because the deism – atheism, really – which he had argued for in Part One of *The Age of Reason*, first published in 1795, had offended Washington and many of his old friends.

Like Byron, Paine was born for opposition, and the causes he especially championed – Democracy and freedom of speech in all matters, including religion, meant that his name was associated with the overthrow of the old order. 'Paine' and 'Painite' were widely used terms of opprobrium. Small children could be threatened by their parents with the promise that acts of misbehaviour would bring the monster, Tom Paine, to their door. *The Rights of Man* had been Paine's reply to Burke's *Reflections*, and at its heart was an argument in favour of cutting down the tree of state whose 'natural' growth Burke had identified and eloquently endorsed. For Crabbe to have Peter 'prove his Freedom and assert the Man' by defying his father with 'Oath and furious Speech' is therefore to sardonically give Peter a specious justification for his determination to go his own way.

This is the way of selfish greed. Peter doesn't give a damn about how he comes by money. 'He fished by water and he filched by land'. And, 'With greedy eye he looked on all he saw,/He knew not Justice and he laughed at Law'. Peter is outside the law, a kind of feral being. He builds a mud hovel, lives as an outcast, but wants 'A feeling creature subject to his power.' Peter is a petty tyrant in search of someone to bully and intimidate. He takes a 'parish-boy' – that is, an orphan, condemned to the workhouse where such children were sent to be under the 'care' of the parish and from where they were off-loaded by those who sold them on for 'a trifling sum', without much by way of enquiry into the fitness of their employers, who were, to all intents and purpose, slave owners.

Oliver Twist, subtitled *The Parish Boy's Progress*, is the most famous work about the brutality of a system which still disfigured the England about which Dickens was writing in the 1830s. There is not much doubt that at least some of the inspiration for his novel came from Letter XXII of *The Borough*. Oliver, a child of 'gentle' nature – the connection between innate characteristics and class status is woven into Dickens' account of him – has a possible antecedent in the third of Peter's apprentices. The first is beaten to death while Peter's neighbours maintain an aloof distance, though 'some, on hearing cries,/Said calmly, "Grimes is at his exercise."' The second is said to have fallen to his death, his body found among the fish in the hold of Peter's boat. Peter is cleared at the subsequent enquiry into the cause of the boy's death. The boy was idle, he says, and was playing when he '"climbed the mainmast and then fell below", – /Then showed his corpse and pointed to the blow./... So they dismissed him, saying at the time,/"Keep fast your Hatchway when you've boys who climb."'

The citizens of the Borough are deftly caught in their cool indifference to the deaths of these two boys. But then comes a third, 'of manners soft and mild' whom all, including '(the poor themselves)' think must be 'Of gentle blood, some noble sinner's son./... he seemed a gracious lad,/In grief submissive and with patience sad.' 'Noble sinner': Crabbe's saturnine wit is recruited to point up prejudice and the unstated snobbishness of those who now turn against Peter when he misuses the boy. The benighted poor, even, consider this boy as more deserving of sympathetic care than Peter's previous apprentices. So when he falls overboard in a rough sea – did he slip or was he pushed to his death by the drunken skipper? – Peter is finally called to account. He is forbidden from hiring further parish boys.

So far the poem has been a mordant, laconic account of the casual brutality of a community which, with few exceptions, takes for granted the exploitation and violent treatment of those with no rights of their own. This is as far as possible from sentimental or picturesque accounts of rural life, its disenchanted realism a rebuke to the evasions of such accounts, whether visual or verbal. But at this point Letter XXII moves into a new phase. The focus shifts from the social to the psychological. Peter, now an outcast, is abandoned to isolation.

> Alone he rowed his boat, alone he cast
> His nets beside, or made his anchor fast;
> To hold a rope, or hear a curse was none –
> He toiled and railed, he groaned and swore alone.

And now Peter's thoughts and perceptions are forced inward. 'Thus by himself compelled to live each day' he finds himself unconsciously absorbing the 'same dull views'. What follows is an absolute *tour-de-force* of descriptive poetry which is so much more than merely descriptive. This, you feel, is what Crabbe has been preparing for through all the years of keen observation of nature. What Peter sees, day after day, profoundly affects his being.

One way of characterising the import of the lines that follow is to say that they are Crabbe's version of the blasted heath in *King Lear*. We know that Crabbe was familiar with the play because he uses a line and a half from it as epigraph for the tale of Ellen Orford: 'Patience and sorrow strove/Who should express her goodliest.' The heath where the outcast Lear finds himself to be 'unaccommodated man ... a poor, bare, forked animal.' In 'Peter Grimes' the heath becomes the sea-shore. This is where Grimes, altogether less eloquent than Lear, finds himself to be face to face with unredeemed, graceless nature. Here, he sees

> The bounding marsh-bank and the blighted tree;
> The water only, when the tides were high,
> When low, the mud half-covered and half-dry;
> The sun-burnt tar that blisters on the planks,

And bank-side stakes in their uneven ranks;
Heaps of entangled weeds that slowly float
As the tide rolls by the impeded boat.

When tides were neap, and in the sultry day,
Through the tall bounding mud-banks made their way,
Which on each side rose swelling, and below
The dark warm flood ran silently and slow;
There anchoring, Peter chose from man to hide,
There hang his head and view the lazy tide
In its hot slimy channel slowly glide;
Where the small eels that left the deeper way
For the warm shore, within the shallows play;
Where gaping mussels, left upon the mud,
Slope their slow passage to the fallen flood; –
Here dull and hopeless he'd lie down and trace
How sidelong crabs had scrawled their crooked race,
Or sadly listen to the tuneless cry
Of fishing gull or clanging golden-eye;
What time the sea-birds to the marsh would come,
And the loud bittern from the bull-rush home
Gave the salt-ditch side the bellowing boom;
He nursed the feelings these dull scenes produce,
And loved to stop beside the opening sluice,
Where the small stream, confined to narrow bound,
Ran with a dull, unvaried, saddening sound,
Where all presented to the eye and ear
Oppressed the soul with misery, grief, and fear.

The scene enters Peter's consciousness, is absorbed into it, becomes inextricably entangled with his sense of abandonment, of utter devastation. (Johnson defined the word as meaning 'waste, havoc, desolation, destruction.') An inarticulate man, he needs Crabbe as interlocutor. Hence, those perhaps anxious moments where the Letter-writer uses such terms as 'dull and hopeless', 'sadly listen', 'saddening sound' – though we should note that Crabbe doesn't say the sound was sad in itself but that it reinforced Peter's sense of misery. What he sees is as much determined by what is going on in his mind as it determines his consciousness. Perception is a two-way process. (A matter treated in comic mode in 'The Lover's Journey' one of the *Tales in Verse*.) To put it rather differently, Peter is not a mere passive observer, his guilt-laden consciousness is a tool of interpretation. As he is, so he sees.

These extraordinary lines are a triumph of the poet's art. There are, for example, the various subtle rhythmic shifts and sonic effects, including echo, assonance, hidden rhyme of 'slope their slow passage to the fallen flood', the clogged movements of 'As the tide rolls by the impeded boat' (where 'tide rolls by' provide a molossus – three stresses together – and the extra syllable drags the line out, a device repeated in 'Ran with a dull, unvaried, saddening sound'); there are the strange emphases on 'Gave the salt-ditch side the bellowing boom', a line which seems to have at least six stresses, there is the way in which sounds reinforce the visual sense of desolation – 'boom' 'clanging' furthering the de-humanised feel of 'The sun-burnt tar that blisters on the planks'; and so on. Wherever you look you see, and by implication hear, a scene utterly bereft of grace.

The last couplet of the passage quoted above is no mere rhetoric. Peter, the opportunistic man of freedom, may like to believe he has no soul – he never says so but this can be inferred from his throwing off of his father's faith – but his soul really is oppressed with misery, grief, and fear. Vicar Crabbe believes in the soul. The poet as psychologist is subtly attuned to the workings of not so much conscience in Peter's case maybe as consciousness. The solitary begins to have visions.

Cold nervous tremblings shook his sturdy frame,
And strange disease – he couldn't say the name.
Wild were his dreams, and oft he rose in fright,
Waked by his view of horrors in the night;
Horrors that would the sternest minds amaze,
Horrors that demons might be proud to raise;
And though he felt forsaken, grieved at heart,
To think he lived from all mankind apart,
Yet if a man approached, in terrors he would start.

In *Mind-Forg'd Manacles* (1987), his magisterial survey of madness in England from the Restoration to the Regency, Roy Porter notes how in the eighteenth century many Christians were oppressed to the point of madness by a sense of 'religious guilt and pollution.' Johnson himself, Christopher Smart, and William Cowper, all in their different ways were for periods of their lives convinced that they were 'isolated, separate, alien, persecuted, cursed.' (pp. 266-7). Crabbe does not intend to link Peter Grimes with these men, but he does want to suggest that Grimes' evil actions bring about an insane belief, enhanced by the desolate world he inhabits, that those he destroyed are in some way taunting him, destroying him in his turn.

When Bill Sikes, the murderer of Nancy in *Oliver Twist*, tries to flee London, he cannot escape from visions of the dead woman, her eyes staring at him. 'If he shut out the sight, there came the room with every well-known object – some, indeed, that he would have forgotten if he had gone over its contents from memory – each in its accustomed place. The body was in *its* place, and its eyes were as he saw them when he stole away.' (ch. 48). There's little doubt that Dickens drew on his reading of Crabbe for this, as he would do later in his account of the brutal murderer Orlick, the lonely haunter of the marshes in *Great Expectations*, a man who harbours resentments against all and who, uncommunicative and sullen, is an image of base, unregenerate human nature, a kind of incorruptible evil. Very like Grimes, in fact.

Peter, by now 'a distempered man', is eventually taken in to 'a parish-bed' and tended by some women who 'perceived compassion on their anger steal.'

In Britten's opera this compassion is softened into near-forgiveness by the imported figure of Ellen Orford, and whoever made this decision adds to the muddle affecting the opera's presentation of the villain-hero. Crabbe makes no such mistake. *His* Peter tells the women ministering to him a tale of visions he has seen, which the Letter-writer says was 'part confession and the rest defence,/A madman's tale with gleams of waking sense.' Peter blurts out how, one day, alone as ever in his boat, he sees his father 'on the water stand/And hold a thin pale boy in either hand/ … I would have struck them, but they knew the intent/And smiled upon the oar, and down they went.' As he talks so, of course, Peter reveals his guilt, which finally leads to a vision of hell as his father and the boys turn the water to flame, throw 'the red-hot liquor' in his face, and force him to look '"Where the flood opened, there I heard the shriek/Of tortured guilt – no earthly tongue can speak:/'All days alike! For ever!' did they say,/'And unremitting torments every day'"'. There is no redemption, not, anyway, one he himself can believe in, for at the very end he cries '"Again they come" and muttered as he died.'

Erasmus Darwin, Crabbe's contemporary with whose two volume *Zoonomia* (1794 and 1796) he would almost certainly have been familiar, argued that as drunkenness made men temporarily out of their wits, prolonged drinking induced insanity. He also asserted, not without reason, that religious fundamentalism was a disease, given that it preyed on the fear of Hell. Methodist preachers, Darwin says, 'successfully inspire this terror, and live comfortably upon the folly of their hearers. In this kind of madness the poor patients frequently commit suicide; although they believe they run headlong into the Hell which they dread!' (*Mind-Forg'd Manacles*, pp. 73-4)

I am not about to suggest that Crabbe treats Peter Grimes as a case-study in drunken delusions fed by religious fundamentalism. Nor does Grimes commit suicide. But his mind is put under pressure and finally broken by forces which both mysteriously come from within – and about which Crabbe is far too tactful to provide an explanation, for that would be reductive – and by other forces which are part of the cultural environment in which Grimes lives, including the religious non-conformity his father surely embraces, and central to which is a crediting of the literal meaning of hellfire and damnation.

'The master-piece of the volume,' Montgomery called 'Letter XXII' of *The Borough*, adding that 'we have been exceedingly struck by the peculiar and unrivalled skill with which Mr Crabbe paints the horrors of a disordered imagination.' Montgomery supposes that such skill may be connected to Crabbe's 'mournful privilege' in watching 'the emotions and [hearing] the ravings of the insane.' (CH, p.105). But even if this is so, many doctors and some vicars must have similarly watched and heard. Only Crabbe created Peter Grimes.

IX

Orford, Keene, and Grimes are written about in Letters which belong to a section called 'The Poor', and the fact that each is so different from the other tells you something about Crabbe's refusal to settle for generalisation, his feeling for difference, for an anti-determinist account of individuality. In the nineteenth century this kind of accounting becomes associated with prose fiction as the novel developed in England, although in a number of uniquely powerful dramatic verse monologues Browning provided vivid, penetrating explorations of individuals who range from unchallengeable piety to outright villainy, with many shades in between. But, I want to say, it all starts with Crabbe.

And even in the two Letters which bring *The Borough* to a close, there is matter which later writers can draw on for their own work. 'Prisons' (Letter XXIII) and, finally, 'Schools', are notable not so much for the details which Crabbe drew on in his writing about the institutions – though that is considerable – but for the fact that he does so without either the sensationalism that had gone with earlier accounts of prisons, or the sentimentality which, from Shenstone's *The Schoolmistress* (1737) to Goldsmith's *Deserted Village*, was habitual to accounts of rural schools.

Crabbe's prisons are not filled merely with rogue criminals – highwaymen, counterfeiters, swindlers – but debtors who themselves are of different kinds. Some mean to cheat, others, though, 'truly strive/To keep their sinking credit long alive:/Success, nay prudence, they may want, but yet/They would be solvent, and deplore a debt'. It might be the epigraph for William Dorrit.

But the ending of the poem is something else. The last prisoner Crabbe writes about is a condemned couple, of whom the woman is in many respects a female version of Grimes.

> She was a pauper bound, who early gave
> Her mind to vice and doubly was a slave;
> Upbraided, beaten, held by rough control,
> Revenge sustained, inspired, and filled her soul:
> She fired a full-stored barn, confessed the fact,
> And laughed at law and justified the act:
> Our gentle vicar tried his powers in vain,
> She answered not, or answered with disdain;
> Th'approaching fate she heard without a sigh,
> And neither cared to live nor feared to die.

Not so much Grimes, perhaps, as a female Bernadine ('A dissolute Prisoner' according to the Dramatis Personae of *Measure for Measure.*) Unregenerate, brute nature.

But her male accomplice is of a different stripe. Terrified of approaching death, he sinks into lethargy, then rouses himself to plead for mercy, fails in his plea, and towards the end seeks refuge in dreams of his earlier life, when he and the girl he then loved were together, free to wander about the countryside at their own sweet will. Crabbe piles on the detail, the stuff of the condemned man's dreams as he, his sister and his 'village-friend', find themselves on the sea-shore and

> search for crimson weeds, which spreading flow
> Or lie like pictures on the sand below;
> With all these bright red pebbles that the sun
> Through the small waves so softly shines upon,
> And those live lucid jellies which the eye
> Delights to trace as they swim glittering by;
> Pearl-shells and rubied star-fish they admire,
> And will arrange above the parlour-fire, –
> Tokens of bliss! – 'Oh, horrible! A wave
> Roars as it rises – save me, Edward, save!'
> She cries. Alas, the watchman on his way
> Calls and lets in – truth, terror, and the day!

The day, that is, of his execution. A great last line and legitimately derived from the fractured dream. I don't know that anyone before Crabbe had made such extraordinary dramatic use of the way in which sounds from the waking world are often incorporated into the world of dreams, nor of how the dreamer tries to accommodate these sounds to the dream narrative until their intrusive presence becomes too strong to resist.

As for the Report on Schools, which is rather how Letter XXIV reads, it begins with the writer claiming that 'To every class we have a School assign'd,/Rules for all ranks and food for every mind', and proves the assertion by a rather dutiful plod through the Borough's educational establishments, although there are signs of life in the account of the lines on Reuben Dixon, who 'has the noisiest school/Of ragged lads, who ever bow'd to rule;/Low in his price – the men who heave our coals,/And clean our causeways, send him boys in shoals'. But by and large you feel that Crabbe's heart isn't really in this Letter. He writes it because he is determined to give his readers a full fig account of the Borough's institutions.

Only at the end of this last Letter do you feel he's much involved in what he says, and even this apologia for his verse feels a bit po-faced. He remarks that he sees it as his duty to combat 'Man's Vice and Crime ... But to his God and conscience leave the man/ ... Yet as I can, I point the powers of rhyme,/And, sparing criminals, attack the crime.' This lacks the hauteur of Pope's 'Ask you what provocation I have had?/The strong antipathy of good to bad', and on the whole I wish Crabbe hadn't bothered with his closing defence of why he writes, especially as *The Borough* has revealed that he is prompted to write for quite different reasons from those he speaks up for at the end of this remarkable work.

Crabbe isn't a routine moralist, he isn't to be thought of as 'Pope in worsted stockings', not fairly, anyway. He is not therefore to be identified as, let alone written off as, a late Augustan. David Hartley (1705-1757) had asserted that his doctrine of 'Association of Ideas' could explain most 'laws' of perception in terms of the connection between how/what a man is and how/what he sees. (A banker gazing on the sun is likely to think of a golden guinea, is scarcely a parodic version of Associationism.) But Crabbe's explorations of projective, subjective, responsive kinds of perception, his probing of the various, often elusive ways a mind works, owes little or nothing to that still prevailing orthodoxy, one which, for example,

Coleridge, Crabbe's younger contemporary, clung to as a young man and only slowly gave up as he became increasingly convinced of the imagination's primary, transformative power.

Crabbe wouldn't have put the matter in Coleridgean terms. But then he didn't need to. His exploration of Peter Grimes' psychology takes him to places neither Coleridge, nor Coleridge's later law-giver, Wordsworth, go. This is among those features, including, for example, the handling of dialogue and the steady control of narrative, which make *The Borough* so remarkable a poem, one I think is a key work in English literature. And Crabbe's next publication shows him to be more remarkable still.

5

Tales in Verse (1812)

I

In contrast with the reviews that greeted the publication of *The Borough*, those that welcomed Crabbe's next book make for depressing reading. Not because they are adversely critical. Though there was some carping, commentators on *Tales in Verse* were for the most part enthusiastic. They also seem to me obtuse or, if that seems too severe, then unaware of what is truly innovative about his newest work. Crabbe is praised for doing those things at which he'd already shown himself adept. It is as though, faced with *Tales in Verse*, the critics clicked into automatic mode. Jeffrey goes so far as to say that Crabbe is repeating himself. 'The pieces before us are ... mere supplementary chapters to *The Borough*, or *The Parish Register*. The same tone – the same subjects – the same style, measure, and versification.' True, Jeffrey then partly redeems himself by finding in the new work virtues and vices which he enumerates as

> the same finished and minute delineation of things
> quite ordinary and common, – generally very engaging
> when employed upon external objects, but often
> fatiguing when directed to insignificant characters and
> habits; – the same strange mixture too of feelings that
> tear the heart and darken the imagination, with starts
> of low humour and patches of ludicrous imagery; –
> the same kindly sympathy with the humble and
> innocent pleasures of the poor and inelegant, and the

same indulgence for the venial offences, contrasted with a strong sense of their frequent depravity, and too constant a recollection of the sufferings it produces, – and, finally, the same honours paid to the delicate affections and noble passions of humble life, with the same generous testimony to their frequent existence, mixed up as before with a reprobation sufficiently rigid, and a ridicule sufficiently severe, of their excesses and affections. (CH, p.164)

This manages to be perceptive about many of Crabbe's virtues while entirely ignoring all that is different about the twenty-one Tales that make up a work even longer than *The Borough*, and which represents, therefore, a prodigious amount of work. And when you consider that, quite apart from his pastoral duties, Crabbe was a family man, and there is no evidence that he shirked any of his responsibilities in either capacity, he must have been working at a kind of white heat of inspiration to have completed so substantial an amount of work between 1810 and 1812.

White heat? It may at first seem ludicrous to apply such a phrase to a writer who never made the kind of claims for himself that were being at that time made by Wordsworth and Coleridge for *their* work, and which would soon be echoed by Shelley. On the contrary, the substantial Preface Crabbe sets at the head of *Tales*, while in some respects it is, as the editor of the *Critical Heritage* volume says, 'Crabbe's most important statement of his own view of his art', gives little enough away. (See CH, p.147). At a guess, he wrote it in answer to Jeffrey's stated hope that the poet of *The Borough*, having proved himself a master of the qualities identified in the passage quoted above, would now move to other, grander, themes, and to encompassing 'a little more of the deep and tragically passions', and 'with less jocularity than prevails in the rest of his writings – rather more incidents – and rather fewer details.' (CH, p.164)

Sorry, Crabbe says, no can do. He isn't cut out for writing epic poetry, which he understands others may be expecting of him, but he does suggest that, although in the Tales he has produced, 'much is lost for want of unity of subject and grandeur of design, something is gained by greater variety of incident and more minute display of character, by accuracy of description, and diversity of scene.' And he then moves to attack mode. While writing in epic mode may seem a proper ambition for a poet, the result can often be a let-down. Why? Because a poem of epic proportions runs the risk of disappointing any reader who is neither greatly interested in the characters, the incidents, nor the setting. Crabbe doesn't go so far as to say that most would-be epic poems are in the end pretty boring, but he does slyly make a case for one undoubted advantage which short tales hold over poems of epic proportions. They are soon over. Independent narratives give the reader who hasn't warmed to any one tale the chance to turn to the next with a 'renovation of hope, although he has been dissatisfied, and a prospect of reiterated pleasure should he find himself entertained.' With the epic, on the other hand, readers are in for the long haul. 'No one ever wished it any longer,' Johnson said of *Paradise Lost*, adding, 'It is a work the reader takes up and then lays aside, and forgets to take up again.' Unfair to that particular epic, perhaps, but the following century was littered with poems that aspired to equal length and gravitas, and are justly forgotten.

And then there is the matter of 'the poetic character'. Crabbe quotes the famous lines from *A Midsummer Night's Dream* about how the poet's eye, in a fine frenzy rolling, can body forth things unknown, and his pen give to airy nothing a local habitation and a name. This may be so, but there are, Crabbe suggests, other ways of being a poet. Why deny the title of poet to those 'who address their productions to the plain sense and sober judgement of their Readers, rather than to their fancy and imagination'? I wasn't aware, Crabbe remarks, with caustic wit and entirely proper disdain, that 'by describing, as faithfully as I could, men, manners, and things, I was forfeiting a just title to a name which has been freely granted to many whom to equal and even excel is but very stinted commendation.'

All praise to Arthur Pollard, who reprints this important Preface in his edition of *The Critical Heritage*. It is inexcusably, I think, absent from the Penguin *Crabbe: Selected Poems*, even though Gavin Edwards does include all twenty-one of the *Tales in Verse*. The Preface is a splendidly defiant statement of Crabbe's poetic concerns, and, in its modest way, a justification for how he writes. Part apologia, part declaration of intent, it is as near as he ever comes to setting out his poetic credo.

Not that it saved him from a drubbing by critics who, having insisted on their admiration for his work, then put the knife into much that is integral to its worth.

To take one example: *The Critical Review* praises Crabbe for his descriptive poetry, which is comparable 'to the Dutch school of painting', but then complains that whereas the best painters of that school 'are at least as remarkable for the force, brilliancy and ... *terseness* of their execution, as for the minuteness of detail which is their most prominent quality', the poet 'squanders himself away in tedious and flat circumstantiality.' Besides, there is altogether too much 'blunt ploughman-like familiarity', by which the anonymous critic seems to mean a button-holing directness of address which he suggests disfigures the opening of most of the Tales. As example of this flaw he quotes the openings of no fewer than nine Tales, including 'Grave Jonas Kindred, Sybil Kindred's sire,/Was Six feet high, and look'd six inches higher' (VI, 'The Frank Courtship'), 'To Farmer Moss, in Langar Vale, came down/His only daughter, from her school in town' (Tale VII, 'The Widow's Tale') and 'Of a fair town, where Dr Rack was guide' (Tale IX 'Arabella').

Reader, Randall Jarrell once asked in mock despair at the

obtuseness of critics, 'we'd never make such mistakes, would we?' – before adding, 'No, we'd make quite different ones.' But it's not difficult to imagine that Crabbe would have felt, if not despair, then a profound exasperation with the wrong-headedness of critics of *Tales in Verse*, even those, like Jeffrey, who extolled the book. Why couldn't they see that he wasn't repeating himself, that he wasn't showing the same excellencies as they rightly praised him for having demonstrated in *The Borough*?

Whether or not Crabbe was exasperated by his critics, we ought surely to be. Consider those openings the *Critical Review* derides? What in heaven's name is wrong with them? They are surely exactly what is needed. They are a model of concise information. They get you straight into the Tale. They give you settings, names, occupations (farmer, doctor) and therefore social ambience, or, in the case of Jonas, make pretty clear that the 'grave' man is almost certainly a member of a religious sect and, given that he must enjoy drawing himself up – he 'look'd six inches higher' – is probably a domestic tyrant and a self-satisfied customer, too. And the poet's sardonic wit is trained on the man. 'Higher' isn't an exact rhyme for 'sire', as you pronounce it you have to draw it out to virtually two syllables, have to elongate it, rather as Jonas elongates himself.

It's entirely possible that in his Preface Crabbe did himself no favours by invoking the names of Dryden and Pope as exemplars. They were, or could be thought of, as very old hat. Of his great contemporaries, only Byron had any time for either poet, and Byron's praise, first given in the clumsy satire he published in 1809, *English Bards and Scotch Reviewers*, was at best a mixed blessing. On the other hand, Crabbe's unemphatic insistence that he was concerned with 'minute display of character' and 'accuracy of description' not merely points to strengths in his new work, these particular strengths hint at what is newest about it. *Tales in Verse* is remarkable, is, I'm sure, utterly original in the ways in which Crabbe recognises circumstance – environment, domestic arrangements, class considerations – as shaping forces in the characters about whom he writes. In other words, words that more or less repeat what I have said before but which now carry additional force, the work Crabbe produced in 1812 mark him out as a novelist in verse, a great one at that.

II

To go through the twenty-one Tales in remorseless detail would take far too long. Instead, I want to examine some of them in order to show how Crabbe uses, among much else, dialogue, domestic environment, social arrangements, the clash of personalities, so as to explore how people come to be what they are, which may well involve them and/or us coming to discover that they are other than they initially took themselves to be. The mode of the Tales is most frequently social comedy, hence the fact that women are at the centre of many of the finest of them. I don't know when Crabbe first read Shakespeare, but he must have been deeply absorbed in the work at the time he was writing or at least coming to think about writing his Tales, because each of them bears epigraphs from the Plays, including the least well-known. The opening Tale, 'The Dumb Orators', carries two epigraphs from *King John*, and one from *Henry VI, Part 2*, plays very seldom performed then as now. But *As You Like It* and *Twelfth Night* are also quoted, and in the course of the Tales Crabbe raids most of the comedies for epigraphs.

This is why, having put women at the heart of many of the Tales, he calls so often on the great Shakespearian comedies. Crabbe's heroines fight for their independence, they fight for – and sometimes against – the men they love, they encounter and try to negotiate with those whose social, patriarchal power, threatens them. Women, as I am by no means the first to point out, are inevitably at the centre of Shakespeare's comedies because the rhythm of these plays is one that finally endorses social harmony. Hence the dances with which they end. Women are figured as lovers, mothers, the creators of new life and therefore of social continuity.

Crabbe is not a tragic poet, any more than he is a writer of epics. Peter Grimes is not a tragic figure, *not* because he comes from humble circumstances – the old idea of the tragic hero having to be a man who falls from high estate is irrelevant here – but because he is entirely lacking in the pitiless self-awareness that, were he to possess it, would, in Macbeth's words, shake his single state of man. Though what he does has tragic consequences for others, he is without insight. He cannot, that is, confront his own guilt, even if in his isolation that forces itself in distorted ways into his consciousness.

But Crabbe is a great comic poet in the sense that he writes about how individual lives are linked to, find expression within, the societies in which they move. And as the American philosopher and aesthetician Susanne K. Langer argued many years ago in her *Feeling and Form: A Theory of Art* (1953), the comic rhythm is one that is manifested in social patterns, including the primal ones of birth, marriage, and death. Hence, the centrality of women to the comic rhythm. Hence, Crabbe's writing about women in so many of the Tales, in several of which, indeed, they are the protagonists. Hence, too, I should add, one more reason for Jane Austen's intense admiration of him. His critics might not have realised what was so new about his work, above all *Tales in Verse*. But she, who was much greater than any of them, knew well enough.

III

Here is the opening of Tale VII, 'The Widow's Tale'.

> To Farmer Moss in Langar Vale came down
> His only daughter, from her school in town,
> A tender, timid maid, who knew not how
> To pass a pig-sty, or to face a cow;
> Smiling she came, with pretty talents graced,
> A fair complexion and a slender waist.

The scene is set for a light comedy of manners. The father is old-style, plain-speaking, bluff, no-nonsense, his daughter a high-falutin' young thing who will presumably learn – or be made to – lose her airs and graces. Before the tale is done, it feels safe to assume, she will have learned to smile the other side of her pretty face. Fair complexions and slender waists may do well enough in town (London, presumably), but they have no place in the country.

> Used to spare meals, disposed in manner pure,
> Her father's kitchen she could ill endure;
> Where by the steaming beef he hungry sat,
> And laid at once a pound upon his plate;
> Hot from the field her eager brother seized
> An equal part and hunger's rage appeased;
> The air surcharged with moisture flagged around,
> And the offended damsel sighed and frowned;
> The swelling fat in lumps conglomerate laid,
> And fancy's sickness seized the loathing maid:
> But when the men beside their station took,
> The maidens with them, and with these the cook;
> When one whole wooden bowl before them stood,
> Filled with huge balls of farinaceous food,

With bacon, mass saline, where never lean
Beneath the brown and bristly rind was seen;
When from a single horn the party drew
Their copious draughts of heavy ale and new;
When the coarse cloth she saw, with many a stain,
Soiled by rude hinds who cut and came again, –
She could not breathe; but, with a heavy sigh,
Reined the fair neck, and shut the offended eye;
She minced the sanguine flesh in frustums fine,
And wondered much to see the creatures dine …

Good, rough humour, and given spice by Crabbe's mocking use of sub-Miltonics, the heavy Latinate diction of, for example, 'mass saline', 'sanguine flesh' (meat that is bloody and which the young woman trims into mathematically exact cubes, 'frustums' being – I quote the OED – 'the portion of a solid figure which remains after the upper part has been cut off by a plane parallel to the base'); and, best of all, 'lumps conglomerate' which gives a mad, ponderous dignity to wads of fat, the more so when we note that 'laid' seems to be used intransitively, as though the fat simply laid itself.

The girl begs to cry off. She pleads to be allowed to take her meals elsewhere, 'in the small parlour, if papa thought fit,/And there to dine, to read, to work alone'. This is typical Crabbe. It was part of the arrangement of domestic architecture at the time to provide for such parlours, to give women a room of their own, so to speak, one where they could pursue their domestic activities of sewing, painting, reading. And for these parlours new kinds of furnishings came in: carpets, soft drapes, easy chairs. Such furnishings were specifically aimed at a new class, that of women, ladies rather, who were educated, 'prepared', for a life separate from the higgledy-piggledy 'rough' routines of day-to-day business and farm affairs.

But her father won't hear of her withdrawing from the kitchen table.

'No,' said the Farmer, in an angry tone,
'These are your school-taught airs; your mother's pride
Would send you there, but I am now your guide. –
Arise betimes, our early meals prepare,
And this despatched, let business be your care;
Look to the lasses, let there not be one
Who lacks attention till her tasks be done;
In every household work your portion take,
And what you make not, see that others make;
At leisure times attend the wheel, and see
The whitening web besprinkled on the lea;
When thus employed, should our young neighbour view
A useful lass – you might have more to do!'

The neighbour the farmer has in mind for his daughter to marry is another farmer, Harry Carr, but the prospect of such a marriage fills the girl with dread: 'a Farmer's wife./A slave! a drudge! – she could not, for her life.' The girl, incidentally, is called Nancy, though the narrative more often identifies her as 'Damsel', 'Maiden', 'Lass', or 'Nymph'. And although I don't propose to provide a detailed account of this tale, it is worth noting that by the end of the narrative, the pair, as we might expect, marry and 'She, her neat taste imparted to the Farm,/And he, the improving skill and vigorous arm.'

Improvement is a key word. 'Improving' farmers were those who in the latter half of the eighteenth century used new methods for arable as well as dairy farming, and improvement also meant taking over what had before been common land, hedging it about, and improving, too, their houses, both architecturally and by landscaping. According to the OED 'improvement' as a term meaning 'The turning of land to profit', begins to emerge in the seventeenth century. But by the eighteenth century it was becoming a commonplace for agricultural circumstance. And this is what interests Crabbe.

'The Widow's Tale' begins with an old-style farmer, who eats with his men in the kitchen. Social historians have noted that by the end of the century this had become far less common. More often now, men continued to eat in the kitchen while farmers ate in the dining room. Farmers, we might say, had improved tastes, and these are intrinsic to the social movements that characterise a period when the opportunity for education of children of the newly moneyed became increasingly widespread.

Nancy is unusual in that her education is at her mother's rather than her father's prompting. The schools being developed at this time, which aimed to provide an education for young ladies – that is, an education into lady-like ways – were intended to make daughters sufficiently polished to attract the attention of a superior class of gentleman. Marrying into the gentry was an ambition many newly-rich or moneyed men wished for their daughters. It was a widely shared ambition. Men of city business were as keen on this as their country cousins. A new pride in achievement, which is a new class pride, is characteristic of eighteenth-century England. You can see it in Hogarth's wonderful portrait painting of father, wife, and daughter, the girl, in her fashionable dress, flawless and slightly smug expression, looking somehow apart from her parents because she has a 'finish' they lack. She is clearly the product of some education which has concentrated on 'polish', 'refinement', those desiderata for making a successful marriage – in other words, marrying 'up'. As for the father, his face is not one of smug self-satisfaction, but he does look justly proud of himself.

Not Farmer Moss, however. His name no doubt indicates his nature: not so much lowly, perhaps, as contentedly earthy and rooted in place. No rolling stone, he. *His* ambition is for his daughter to marry one of his own kind and to prepare for this by assuming the kinds of responsibilities which, allowing for social distinction, were neglected by the Lady of the Hall. He is not like Squire Melbury of Hardy's great novel, *The Woodlanders*, who sends his daughter Grace away to school so that she can be educated out of country ways, and who then feels saddened at the social gap that opens up between them. For Farmer Moss there is to be no gap. And though by the end of 'The Widow's Tale' we understand how through improvement changes will come, they don't produce an abrupt fracture of relationship.

This is partly because of the Tale's eponymous widow, whom Nancy seeks out as solace from her father's plan for her. She has heard that the widow made a romantic match but now learns that it foundered for lack of money. Eventually, the woman tells Nancy, she married a man out of a kind of pallid gratitude for his long-suffering love, a love she didn't return, although 'in tranquil ease we passed our latter years,/By griefs untroubled, unassailed by fears.' You can almost see the novelist who wrote *Sense and Sensibility* nodding her approval. Better Colonel Brandon and his flannel waistcoats than Willoughby and his blond good looks. The former can, after all, offer the young, romantic Marianne Dashwood money and security.

'The Widow's Tale' has for one of its epigraphs the moment in *As You Like It* where Rosalind upbraids the country girl Phebe for her cruel rejection of Corin. 'Cry the man mercy, love him take his offer,' she tells her. (Act 3, scene v). Crabbe, sceptical of the advantages of romantic love, sees marriage as a social contract. The marriage of Nancy and Harry Carr is such a contract and it symbolises – if that's not too blatant a term – a subtle adjustment of social circumstance, a Burkean endorsement of 'natural' change which Nancy's education, her 'neat taste', and her husband's 'improving skill' makes possible.

A comic tale, then, but one given substance by the attentive manner in which Crabbe writes about the social realities which do so much to shape the lives of the tale's characters. In its relaxed, even minor mode, 'The Widow's Tale' tells you a good deal about what was going on in England at the time, and it does it without heavy-handed moralising or the dull accumulation of detail of which Crabbe has so often and so unfairly been accused.

It also contrasts interestingly with Tale III, 'The Gentleman Farmer'. For in that tale, Gwyn, the farmer in question, is shown to be anything but old style. He is not merely an 'improving' farmer, he is *au fait* with the latest developments, and quick to mock those who cling to old-style routines 'when not a man had seen/Corn sown by Drill, or threshed by a Machine!' Gwyn is an instance of a new breed of farmer. Such farmers were owners of large swathes of land, most of it acquired by supplanting small farms and enclosing tracts of common land. Gwyn is one of those whose

> skill assigns the prize
> For creatures fed in pens, and stalls, and styes,
> And who, in places where Improvers meet,
> To fill the land with fatness, had a seat;
> Who in large mansions live like petty kings,
> And speak of farms as but amusing things;
> Who plans encourage, and who journals keep,
> And talk with lords about a breed of sheep.

Gwyn is aware of the innovations brought about by such as Jethro Tull, whose seed drill entirely changed sowing routines, and whose treatises on agricultural methods, together with the work of Arthur Young, advanced ways of planting crops. Nor is that all. Crabbe tells us that 'Fixed in his farm, he soon displayed his skill/In small-boned lambs, the Horse-hoe, and the drill.' As a gentleman farmer, Gwyn fancies himself not merely as a cultivator of the land but as a breeder of livestock – the kind from whom artists, pre-eminently William Stubbs, but also a host of lesser names, could gain well-paid commissions portraying them beside a prize bull or ram or stallion in those many genre paintings that were turned out to flatter the newly wealthy hobby farmers – for that is what they were – who emerge in the latter half of the eighteenth century. Such paintings were, and often still are, to be found hung on the walls of country houses and manor farms.

Crabbe distinguishes between two types of gentleman farmer. There is the farmer who, having made money from his work, 'rides his hunter, who his house adorns,/Who drinks his wine and his disbursements scorns'. This is the farmer 'made the gentleman'. But Gwyn belongs to the other type, who chooses to retire from city living to take up farming 'solely by a passion led/Or by a fashion; curious in his land,/Now planning much, now changing what he planned.' This type is the 'Gentleman. A farmer made.' Between them, the two types tell a good deal about the fact as well as the nature of social change on the land that was occurring during the period with which Crabbe is concerned.

Needless to say, Farmer Moss belongs to neither category identified in 'The Gentleman Farmer'. He is a man who works, as he eats, alongside his farm labourers, whereas we never hear of those who work on Gwyn's estate. We do, though, hear of how Gwyn 'adorns' his house – which his guests 'politely called a Seat.' ('Mansion, dwelling, residence, abode' – Johnson. Nobody would think of calling Farmer Moss' farmhouse a 'Seat'.) The rooms of Gwyn's 'mansion', we are told, are 'rather fine than neat':

> At much expense was each apartment graced.
> His taste was gorgeous, but it still was taste;
> In full festoons the crimson curtains fell,
> The sofas rose in bold elastic swell;
> Mirrors in gilded frames displayed the tints
> Of glowing carpets and of coloured prints:
> The weary eye saw every object shine,
> And all was costly, fanciful, and fine.

Crabbe rather gives up in that final couplet, as though himself too weary to bother itemising any more of the furnishings that display Gwyn's taste. And the terms he uses quite lack the detail and precision he brings to his description of Dinah's rooms in Tale IV, 'Procrastination', of which more later. Here, it is enough to note that Gwyn the Gentleman Farmer, a man of taste, has scarcely anything in common with Farmer Moss: he is a free-thinker, a self-professed admirer of Hume, Gibbon and Tom Paine, someone who in defiance of what might be called bourgeois morality takes a mistress, elegantly denounces priests, and for a while at least lives 'a sweet harmonious life'. But then the moral code he despises bites back and he falls victim to superstitious dread, marries his mistress, Rebecca, and becomes dependent for the salvation of the soul he did not once believe in on a Methodist. That's what happens if you scorn a reasonable view of religion and its attendant moral imperatives.

None of this is, to be honest, especially interesting. The meat of 'The Gentleman Farmer' is in Crabbe's attention to what the term means. The rest is trivial.

IV

'The Gentleman Farmer' is one of the few Tales that don't take love and marriage as their subject. We know nothing about Gwyn's parents. A man of independent means, this gentleman farmer seems, rather like Gatsby, to have sprung from some Platonic conception of himself. But in most of the Tales parents are not only present, they are crucial forces in shaping the lives of their offspring, especially of the daughters. 'The business of her life was to get her daughters married,' Jane Austen says of Mrs Bennet. A similar business engages lives of most of the parents about whom Crabbe writes. In the absence of his wife,

Farmer Moss has to make Nancy's marriage his business. The mother of the eponymous Tale VIII makes it *her* business to prevent her younger daughter, Lucy, from marrying the man of Lucy's choice.

'The Mother' is a riveting study in female egotism, chilling, even slightly macabre. It begins with a rapid, expertly narrated account of a young beauty, Dorothea, the apple of her parents' eye, who grows up secure on her own sense of worth: 'She wrote a billet, and a novel read,/And with her fame her vanity was fed'. The 'fame' is, it hardly needs to be said, to be understood as a tongue-in-cheek reference to a purely local reputation, but this is sufficient to bring suitors aplenty to Dorothea's door. All but one are sent packing. The one exception is a 'a man so mild' she can bend him to her will with ease. Her parents now dead, she agrees to his proposal of marriage, makes his life hell, and 'Twelve heavy years this patient soul sustained/This wasp's attacks, and then her praise obtained,/Graved on a marble tomb, where he at peace remained.' This is Crabbe in his mode of laconic, almost ruthless reporter of human viciousness, one in which, Byron and Jane Austen apart, he has few rivals.

The mother is left with two daughters. The elder, like herself, is a beauty, and therefore, her mother senses, something of a rival. 'The daughter's charms increased, the parent's yet remained.' Lucy, the younger daughter, is without good looks, or so her mother assures her. But though the girl at first weeps for 'her slighted face ... [she] then began to smile at her disgrace.' She goes to live with an aunt – '"Thou art the image of thy pious aunt,"' the mother tells her with unconcealed disdain, and there she is courted by a 'youthful rector', who esteems Lucy for her innate worth.

Lucy seeks her mother's approval for the marriage offer she receives, and though this is at first refused, the mother eventually writes to tell her that she will allow her a small portion of money if she takes it with grateful thanks 'and [waits] the sister's day.' From which we infer that the settlement her father had made on Lucy has almost certainly been appropriated by the mother, but once Lucy's sister is married, Dorothea will, out of the goodness of her heart, permit the girl to have what little is left. But then the sister dies and the mother changes her mind. On no account is Lucy to marry the rector. The aunt speaks up for her and is sent packing. The rector, finding he can make no headway against the domestic tyrant and snob who prevents Lucy from marrying him, eventually settles on another woman, and Lucy decides to die.

There is nothing histrionic about her decision, no swooning fit, no impulse to commit suicide. The mother cannot quite credit what Lucy is about.

> Surprised, the mother saw the languid frame,
> And felt indignant, yet forebore to blame;
> Once with a frown she cried, 'And do you mean
> To die of love – the folly of fifteen?'
> But as her anger met with no reply
> She let the gentle girl in quiet die,
> And to her sister wrote, impelled by pain,
> 'Come quickly, Martha, or you come in vain.'
> Lucy meantime professed with joy sincere
> That nothing held, employed, engaged her here.

At her age, which we can calculate as about thirty, Lucy certainly isn't going to be touched by her mother's suggestion that she is behaving like a fifteen-year-old, knowing, anyway, that the pain which causes the mother to write to her aunt is one of injured pride, not concern for her, Lucy. 'Then grew the soul serene … /Till death approached, when every look expressed/A sense of bliss, till every sense had rest.'

Not that her younger daughter's death bothers the mother.

It gives her a new image to offer to public scrutiny, that of grieving but nobly forbearing woman, one she manages so effectively that 'the astonished throng/Pronounced her peerless as she moved along.' And appropriately enough, the Tale ends with Dorothea studying herself in the mirror.

> Her picture then the greedy dame displays,
> Touched by no shame, she now demands its praise;
> In her tall mirror then she shows her face,
> Still coldly fair with unaffecting grace;
> These she compares, 'It has the form,' she cries,
> 'But wants the air, the spirit, and the eyes;
> This as a likeness is correct and true,
> But there alone the living grace we view.'
> This said, the applauding voice the dame required,
> And, gazing, slowly from the glass retired.

It is an astonishing, hair-raising conclusion. This is egotism raised to the power of evil. By what feels like an uncanny coincidence Grimm's Tales began to appear in 1812, though I don't intend to suggest an influence in either direction, for that would have been an impossibility. It is more that Crabbe brings an awful psychological plausibility to this study of the archetypal wicked mother. Having her compare her portrait with the mirror-image and then provide her own approving words, 'the applauding voice', to what she perceives to be the truth-telling power of portraiture, 'the living grace' it allots her, is a master stroke. Dorothea becomes the audience of her own appearance, able to judge that the mirror provides only 'unaffecting grace'. It is, of course, a terrible truth, though not one she can bring herself to acknowledge. All she can say is that the image she sees in the glass cannot move her. Its grace is physical only. What she hungers to witness is 'grace' in its spiritual dimension, such as the portrait supplies. That the syntax is so knotty is essential to what Crabbe is doing. The mother can't, that is, plainly confront the truth of her terrible sterility. She is like a female version of Henry James' Dr Sloper, of *Washington Square*, who wrecks his daughter's life by the ferocious, undeflectable power of his egotistic self-centredness and self-referentiality. 'The Mother' is a great poem and I am staggered that it hasn't been recognised as such.

V

An egotism very similar to Dorothea's seems to be on display in Tale VI, 'The Frank Courtship', where a father wants to insist his daughter marry the man he has chosen for her. The tale's *donnée* is, in other words, similar to that of 'The Widow's Tale', but the setting is very different.

> Grave Jonas Kindred, Sybil Kindred's sire,
> Was six feet high, and looked six inches higher,
> Erect, morose, determined, solemn, slow,
> Who knew the man, could never cease to know;
> His faithful spouse, when Jonas was not by,
> Had a firm presence and a steady eye,
> But with her husband dropped her look and tone,
> And Jonas ruled unquestioned and alone.

These are the masterly opening lines of one of the greatest of the Tales. 'The Frank Courtship' is so wonderful that the temptation is simply to quote and go on quoting the entire five hundred lines that make up the Tale. Johnson defines 'morose' as meaning 'sour of temper, peevish', but Crabbe probably intends some of its earlier connotations to cling to the word. Ben Jonson was famously called 'morose', and the epithet was intended to convey that great writer's unwavering, scrupulous, painstaking seriousness in the pursuit of his calling. In other words, the term was meant more as compliment than criticism, and though Crabbe certainly wants us to recognise Jonas' heavy insistence on his own moral stringency, he doesn't intend to make mock of the man.

His daughter, however, does. Or rather, being as high spirited as her father, Sybil is as equally determined to follow whatever course of action she sets herself; she is not prepared to adopt her mother's submissive stance. Jones may rule his wife, 'unquestioned and alone' (that final word suggests the lack of sexual warmth, of reciprocity, as well as lack of companionship, between the couple), but Sybil has no intention of doing her father's bidding, not, at all events, if it doesn't coincide with her own inclinations. At first this doesn't seem a problem, because 'Sybil then was in that playful time/When contradiction is not held a crime', but it will become one when she fails to acknowledge that her father not merely rules unquestioned and alone but 'bids all murmurs, all objections cease,/And with imperious voice, announces – Peace!'

As the name Jonas Kindred implies, the father and his family are strict puritans. They belong, we are told, to 'that crew,/Who, as their foes maintain, their Sovereign slew ... Cromwell was still their saint'. And then follows one of Crabbe's great set pieces, in which he describes the Kindred household. Too long to quote in its entirety, it is a further example of why, as with much else of his work, the nineteenth-century novelists so admired him. Nobody before Crabbe had written about domestic arrangements, about furnishings, décor, the daily appurtenances of living, with the kind of detail he does, detail that makes substantial, psychologically as well as physically, the lives of those who fill his poems. This isn't detail for the sake of it. If, as a later poet says, 'How we live measures our own nature', then Crabbe has a fair claim to be regarded as the first poet to provide the means for such measurement.

Here he is, then, describing with an almost Dickensian attentiveness, the Kindreds at home:

> Fixed were their habits; they arose betimes,
> Then prayed their hour, and sang their party-rhymes;
> Their meals were plenteous, regular, and plain,
> The trade of Jonas brought him constant gain;
> Vendor of Hops and Malt, of Coals and Corn,
> And like his father, he was Merchant born.
> Neat was their house, each table, chair, and stool,
> Stood in its place, or moving, moved by rule;
> No lively print or picture graced the room;
> A plain brown paper lent its decent gloom;
> But here the eye, in glancing round, surveyed
> A small recess that seemed for china made;
> Such pleasing pictures seemed this pencilled ware
> That few would search for nobler objects there –
> Yet, turned by chosen friends, and there appeared
> His stern, strong features whom they all revered;
> For there in lofty air was seen to stand
> The bold Protector of the conquered land …
>
> There stood a clock, though small the owner's need,
> For habit told when all things should proceed.
> Few their amusements, but when Friends appeared,
> They with the world's distress their spirits cheered …
> Their town was large, and seldom passed a day
> But some had failed and others gone astray;
> Clerks had absconded, wives eloped, girls flown
> To Gretna-Green, or sons rebellious grown;
> Quarrels and fires arose! – and it was plain
> The times were bad; the Saints had ceased to reign!

Crabbe has a note to explain that when he uses the term Saints it is 'not ironically or with malignity; but it is taken merely to designate a morosely devout people, with peculiar austerity of manners.'

Sybil escapes from the morose and austere Kindred household when her father sends her to the care of his sister. This device of parcelling a young woman off to a near relation or in some instances a rich family friend occurs so often in the Tales that we may be tempted to doubt whether, for all the variations Crabbe plays it, the gimmick can bear so much repetition. But in fact it was the traffic of the time, because it was seen as an acceptable way of allowing a young woman to gain some experience of the world before taking up her duties as wife and mother. It was, if not exactly a finishing school, a way of adding polish to marriageable property.

But in Sybil's case, as with other young women in the Tales, it proves to be a dangerous move. The sister introduces her niece to a lively social scene:

> All here was gay and cheerful – all at home
> Unvaried quiet and unruffled gloom;
> There, were no changes, and amusements few –
> Here, all was varied, wonderful, and new;
> There, were plain meals, plain dresses, and grave looks –
> Here, gay companions and amusing books,
> And the young beauty soon began to taste
> The light vocations of the scene she graced.

It's perhaps a pity that in comparison to the splendidly evocative account of the Kindred household and its regulated ways Crabbe here offers few details of the aunt's domestic circumstances or her social round ('wonderful' is a woeful space-filler), but anyway the real action is happening at home, where the father bids his sister bring Sybil every year so he can measure her progress. The aunt has no problem with this. They will go, she tells her niece, '"and by our dress/A grave conformity of mind express,/Must sing at Meeting, and from cards refrain,/The more to enjoy when we return again."' The rhythmic skip on the second foot here – 'to enjoy' is an anapest – deftly implies the enjoyment that comes from fooling Jonas. Not that this is entirely to Sybil's taste. For 'Vain as she was – and flattery made her vain – /Her simulation gave her bosom pain.'

Besides, she begins to tire of the social whirligig, preferring to spend some hours alone, reading or walking, 'Pleased with the pensive gloom and evening bird' – presumably the nightingale. But the real test comes when, once she has returned home, Jonas tells his daughter he has chosen a husband for her. He has already spoken to his wife about this: '"You shall advise the maiden, I will threat;/Her fears and hopes may yield us comfort yet."' Clearly, Jonas is not as confident he can bend Sybil to his will as he wants to appear. And it is now, through dialogue, that Crabbe comes to the real meat of his tale.

First, Jonas tells Sybil that the youth he has chosen to be her husband is '"one I approve"' and that she must therefore '"prepare to honour and love"' him. Should she not do so, should she show him rudeness, or '"treat him with disdain … Or of one taunting speech give certain proof,/Girl! I reject thee from my sober roof."' 'Girl!' The word is intended to show Sybil that she is no match for her father.

But she is.

> 'My aunt,' said Sybil, 'will with pride protect
> One whom a father can for this reject;
> Nor shall a formal, rigid, soulless boy
> My manners alter or my views destroy.'

Touché. Calling her prospective husband 'Boy!' is a sure way to show her contempt for what her father proposes. It's too much for Jonas who 'uttering something between a sigh and groan' leaves his wife to try to reason with Sybil.

The consequence of this is a most revealing speech. The mother begs Sybil to take the youth her father wants her to marry. Why? Because he is 'mild'. Having said which, she reveals the state of her own marriage.

> 'Thy father, Sybil, never could be moved
> By one who loved him, or by one he loved.
> Union like ours is but a bargain made
> By slave and tyrant – he will be obeyed,
> Then calls the quiet, comfort – but thy Youth
> Is mild by nature, and as frank as truth.'

The mother's words are both touching and, and in her attempt to reconcile Sybil to what she imagines will be her daughter's lot, desperately sad. And yet though Jonas is, it's plain, a domestic tyrant, he is not being caricatured as a Bounderby-type of bone-headed egotist. Because, as is also plain, he is a man who loves his family, and according to his lights wants to behave well by them.

Besides, he has some right on his side. The mother shares his fear of what she calls '"That dangerous love by which the young are led."' '"Can eyes and feelings inward worth descry?"' she asks, and in doing so speaks for other protagonists of *Tales in Verse* who find themselves beguiled by their heart's impulses, the allure of a pretty face or a handsome profile, into unsuitable, imprisoning and degrading marriages. This is, supremely, Jane Austen territory, and she would agree with the closing plea which Sybil's mother makes to her daughter: '"Yield but esteem, and only try for peace."'

'Esteem' is a word that runs through the *Tales*. The most

plangent use of the term probably occurs in the opening lines of Tale IV, 'Procrastination': 'Love will expire – the gay, the happy dream,/Will turn to scorn, indifference, or esteem'. Johnson defines the noun as meaning 'high value; reverential regard', and although we might think 'reverential' is pitching it too high, to find someone worthy of esteem certainly involves true judgement, reasonable assessment.

Here, then, it will help to consider two of the epigraphs that head 'The Frank Courtship'. They are from *Much Ado About Nothing*, the comedy which features the 'merry war of wits' between Beatrice and Benedick. (In passing, I should note that the way Crabbe uses epigraphs taken from Shakespeare reveals not only his wide knowledge of the plays but the depth of his understanding of them. You could write a good commentary on Shakespeare taking as starting point Crabbe's quotations and how they relate to his *Tales*.) The two major characters of *Much Ado About Nothing* are brilliantly intelligent, hard-headed and, it turns out, warm-hearted, reluctant lovers, who in knocking spots off each other come to acknowledge painful truths about themselves. Theirs is the most reasonable of loves. The key moment in the play, their mutual acknowledgement of this comes in Act 5, scene iv, when Benedick asks Beatrice 'Do not you love me?' and she replies, 'Why no, no more than reason.'

For one of the epigraphs to the Tale, Crabbe quotes her earlier lines 'What fire is in my ears; can it be true/Stand I condemned for pride and scorn so much?' But what is sauce for the goose is sauce for the gander, as the lovers in both play and poem discover. Sybil is sublimely confident of her own witty fearlessness. '"I must be loved,"' she tells her mother, '"I must see/The man in terrors who aspires to me."' She is her father's daughter, right enough. Hence, her riposte to her poor mother, who says in appalled wonderment of her proposed suitor, Josiah, '"He kneel and tremble at a thing of dust!/He cannot, Child." – The child replied "he must."' And with this defiant riposte in mind, we can note the appropriateness of the other epigraph from Shakespeare's play: 'Yes, faith, it is my Cousin's duty to make a curtsy, and say "Father, as it please you"; but for all that, Cousin, let him be a handsome fellow, or else make another curtsy and say, "Father, as it pleases me."'

But handsome fellow though Josiah may be, he doesn't choose to supplicate Sybil. When she first sees him, Sybil acknowledges much in his person, including what she can guess is 'A heart unspotted and a life unblamed'. But she also sees in him 'The formal air, and something of the pride/That indicates the wealth it seems to hide;/And looks that were not, she conceived, exempt/From a proud pity, or a sly contempt.' He, in his turn, registers the 'lofty air, that scorn or pride express,/With that insidious look, that seemed to hide/In an affected smile the scorn and pride.'

After which, having silently weighed each other up, they speak, Josiah first. '"Fair maiden, art thou well?" – /"Art thou Physician?" she replied; "my hand,/My pulse at least shall be at thy command."' Beatrice herself could have done no better.

But Josiah discomforts Sybil by immediately kneeling and giving 'his lips the offered pulse to feel'. Sybil attempts to recover her self-composure by asking if he thinks her well, and he replies that '"I, in thy light luxuriant robe, behold/Want and excess, abounding and yet cold … /Both health and beauty, learned authors show,/From a just medium in our clothing flow."' And, when she begs him to proceed with his diagnosis, he tells her that he can see she is '"enamoured of thyself;/my art/Can see the naughty malice of thy heart."' He then delivers what, in its reproof of her worldliness, amounts to a sermon on the need for modesty, for attending to virtues that will turn her from a world of sin. Josiah, it is clear, is not averse from speaking home truths and speaking them without dissimulation.

Sybil is rattled, but she's also justifiably irritated by what she detects is a certain smugness in his address. He speaks as though at '"Meeting,"' she tells him, adding that '"for a sinner, thou'rt too much a saint."' And with some relish she then anatomises *his* faults, including his self-conscious dress and manner of address: '"why should goodness be/Wrapped in a garb of such formality,"' she enquires, for '"what is sound can be/So void of grace as dull monotony?"' Then comes the killer.

'Love has a thousand varied notes to move
The human heart, – thou may'st not speak of love,
Till thou has cast thy formal airs aside,
And those becoming youth and nature tried;
Not till exterior freedom, spirit, ease,
Prove it thy study and delight to please;
Not till these follies meet thy just disdain,
While yet thy virtues and thy worth remain.'

And with this she sends him packing.

The father, having heard what Josiah has to tell him, correctly intuits that the youth loves his daughter, and, this being so, he is particularly keen that his plan that Josiah and Sybil should marry must succeed. He has therefore to confront his daughter.

With anger fraught, but willing to persuade,
The wrathful father met the smiling maid:
'Sybil,' said he, 'I long, and yet I dread
To know thy conduct – hath Josiah fled?
And, grieved and fretted by thy scornful air,
For his lost peace betaken him to prayer?
Coulds't thou his pure and modest mind distress
By vile remarks upon his speech, address,
Attire and voice?' – 'All this I must confess.'
'Unhappy child! What labour will it cost

To win him back.' 'I do not think him lost.'
'Courts he, then, trifler, into and disdain?'
'No, but from these he courts me to refrain.'
'Then hear me, Sybil, should Josiah leave
Thy father's house – ' 'My father's Child would grieve.'
'That is of grace. And if he come again
To speak of love?' 'I might from grief refrain.'
'Then wilt thou, Daughter, our design embrace?'
'Can I resist it, if it be of grace?'
'Dear Child, in three plain words thy mind express –
Wilt thou have this good youth?' 'Dear Father, yes.'

There are many examples of excellently conducted dialogue throughout the Tales, but this is perhaps the finest of them all. Others make use of the cut and thrust so dazzlingly managed here. For example in Tale XI 'Edward Shore', the eponymous hero/protagonist speaks out of the self-assurance of untested youth when he scornfully repudiates a friend's claim that men can fall into error through temptation. They shouldn't, he says, and temptation, however strong, is no excuse.

'Man's heart deceives him,' said a friend. 'Of course,'
Replied the youth, 'but has it power to force?
Unless it forces, call it as you will,
It is but wish, and proneness to the ill.'

'Art thou not tempted?' 'Do I fall?' said Shore.
'The pure have fallen.' 'They are pure no more … '

Needless to say, by the end of the tale, Shore has fallen into an adulterous love affair and, appalled by his own behaviour, becomes a man so unsure of himself (the pun on his name is unmissable) that he loses his reason and becomes a grotesque parody of childishness. 'Simple and weak, he acts the boy once more,/And heedless children call him Silly Shore.'

The argument between young Shore and his friend is superbly managed, the arrogant young man's certainties neatly established by rhyme and line ending. And there are many other instances in the Tales of Crabbe's masterly way with dialogue, his ability to manoeuvre the formal properties of the couplet so as to give point and dramatic edge to speech. But the closing exchange between father and daughter of 'The Frank Courtship' is unsurpassable. Wonderful, the way Sybil lets her father rant on about her presumed offence in chastising Josiah for his ways, then say merely '"All this I must confess."' Though Jonas insists on his own power and authority, it is she who holds all the cards. And they both know it. So when the father expostulates about the labour that will have to be expended in bringing Josiah again – *his* labour, he means, *his* cost – she replies '"I do not think him lost."' She knows what her father doesn't, that Josiah, is drawn to her by her very independence, her spirited refusal to succumb at once to him. This is, of course, what draws Benedick to Beatrice.

Part of Sybil's spiritedness lies in her dazzling wit. Her father, with some pomposity, tells her that admitting she might grieve if Josiah were lost is a sign of grace, and then, when he asks her if she will after all accept his proposal for a marriage with Josiah, she says, '"Can I resist it, if it be of grace?"' The remark is at once playful and entirely serious. The hint of mockery that throws the word back at him is also an acceptance that the marriage *is* of grace. And it is then, for the first time, we realise, that Jonas, with his own good grace, accepts that Sybil is his equal. The clue is in the term of endearment. '"*Dear Child.*"' (My italics) He has never called her that before. And it draws from her the return endearment. '"Dear father"'. A meeting of minds, a marriage of minds. Esteem.

VI

As I have already noted that word esteem occurs at the opening of another of the great Tales, 'Procrastination', but here it is honoured in the breech. A meeting of minds precedes a parting, and this leads to an abandoned marriage. 'Procrastination' is a magnificently told story of the ways in which material consideration takes hold of a person's mind. In some ways therefore it anticipates Tale XX, 'The Brothers', where the protagonists, George and his brother Isaac, grow apart, because George, having handed over his share of the money the two of them inherited from their fisherman father, goes away to sea rather than waiting to be impressed, and is soon engaged in battle. This, by the way, is one of Crabbe's few allusions to the conflicts that beset the Napoleonic period, though like Jane Austen he nearly always presents sailors in a favourable light.

Years later, having by now lost a leg, George finally returns to take up a berth in his brother's house. Meanwhile, his brother, 'weak, attentive, slow, exact', makes the kind of marriage that helps advance his worldly prospects, and feels a growing resentment at his brother's return, one intensified by his wife's steely dislike, since, with his smoking and drinking, George lowers the tone of the place where the pair rejoice in entertaining snobbish neighbours. Only their son, also a George, shows the old salt any kindness, and his parents warn him off his uncle, who dies a sad and lonely death.

But after his brother has gone to his grave, Isaac is wounded by remorseful awareness of how he's neglected his duty as a brother. 'And thus he lives, if living be to sigh,/And from all comforts of the world to fly,/Without a hope in life – without a wish to die.'

The struggles of conscience – the title of Tale XIV – form the basis of many of the Tales, which deal with matters of faith, of works, of guilt and repentance. There can be a routine feel to this, as though Parson Crabbe is doing his duty by his vocation. But more frequently he is deeply and tellingly engaged with such matters.

Hence, the mordant Tale XV, 'Advice; or The Squire and the Priest', which has an almost Chaucerian regard for the ways in which a man tries to ease his conscience by getting a carefully-chosen priest who is mindful of the requirements of the flesh to minister to him. And in both this and other Tales Crabbe writes searchingly about the subtle negotiations the clergy need to make between what might be called the requirements of the parish and duty to God. But he is also someone whose deep fascination with the way the mind works makes for a non-doctrinaire recognition of human variety and of the unaccountable mysteries of behaviour.

And yet though behaviour may be unaccountable, Crabbe doesn't rely on the mysterious workings of grace to explain all. On the contrary, the characters about whom he writes are responsible for their lives. They *choose*. Against this, however, they are tied, or at least conditioned, by conventions, by money or the lack of it – especially in the case of his many women protagonists, who are further constrained by class, by looks, by education, by, in short, all those considerations out of which the great nineteenth-century fiction writers will make their novels.

Tale XIII, 'Jesse and Colin' is a kind of pastoral – a rare event in Crabbe – in which a couple are parted by the death of the young woman's father, a Vicar, as a result of which she goes to live with a rich woman friend, very much, as has already been noted, as girls in other of the Tales have to do. But instead of what might be expected, a final sundering of their relationship, the couple in this Tale come together again. Jesse is increasingly put upon by her apparent saviour, who orders her to spy on her servants. When Jesse refuses to do so, she is treated as Lady

Catherine de Bourgh treats all who oppose her. There is, as we might expect, a passage of brilliantly managed dialogue between the Dame and Jesse, in which the Dame cajoles, wheedles, and then, when these tactics fail, insults and tries to humiliate the girl.

But all to no avail. Jesse returns home, unsure what she will find, but Colin and she are re-united and, despite his fears that she will have grown used to 'Grandeur and taste', Jesse

> In the mild evening, in the scene around,
> The Maid, now free, peculiar beauties found;
> Blended with village-tones, the evening-gale
> Gave the sweet night-bird's warblings to the vale.
> The youth emboldened, yet abashed, now told
> His fondest wish, nor found the maiden cold;
> The mother smiling whispered – 'Let him go
> And seek the licence!' Jesse answered 'No':
> But Colin went. – I know not if they live
> With all the comforts wealth and plenty give,
> But with pure joy to envious souls denied,
> To suppliant meanness and suspicious pride;
> And village maids of happy couples say,
> 'They live like Jesse Bourn and Colin Grey.'

Tales of rural contentment, of long-lived married couples, belong within the tradition of pastoral which in the eighteenth century can be traced back to the proverbial Darby and Joan. The ballad story of this ideal couple, by Henry Woodfall, celebrated the life of Woodfall's employer, John Darby, who died in 1730, and of his wife. But the tradition itself stretches back through the shepherd and his wife in *The Winter's Tale* – she is dead but lovingly remembered as a model of welcoming hospitality – to one of the most touching of Ovid's *Metamorphoses*, the tale of Baucis and Philemon, a humble couple who offer to share what food and drink they have with the poor travellers arrived unexpectedly at their door. The travellers are in fact gods in disguise, one of them Jupiter, who is so delighted by the couple's hospitality that he immediately erects a temple on the spot of their cottage, makes them its custodians, and grants them their wish to die in the same hour, after which they are transformed into trees that grow in each other's shade. In Michael Longley's beautiful re-telling of this moment, which can be found in *After Ovid: New Metamorphoses*, edited by Michael Hofmann and James Lasdun, we are told that

> At the end of their days when they were very old and bowed
> And living on their memories, outside the chapel door
> Baucis who was leafy too watched Philemon sprouting leaves.
> As tree-tops overgrew their smiles they called in unison
> 'Goodbye my dear.' Then the bark knitted and hid their lips.

VII

This tradition of the couple whose mutual contentment goes hand-in-hand with indifference to social forms is one to which Crabbe bows in 'Jesse and Colin', and it is, perhaps, implicit in Tale XVIII, 'The Wager'. Here, two partners in trade, having done well out of their business affairs, decide to marry. Counter will, he says, take a wife he can control. Clubb wants a wife he can respect. Clubb is the happier but, in a neat twist, Counter finds his wife's submissiveness exercises a control over him he had not anticipated. Mrs Counter may not be capable of deep feeling but she wins because she is of the type who 'drooping ... seek your pity to excite/ ... They are like ice that in the hand we hold,/So very melting, yet so very cold'. Here is no marriage of true minds, and therefore no true marriage. Impossible to imagine them together in that mutuality of regard which the relationship of Baucis and Philomen signifies, or, of course, that of Jesse and Colin.

Separation of lovers is, however, often enforced. Tale II, 'The Parting Hour', begins with the narrator inviting us to observe 'an ancient pair'

> A sleeping man; a woman in her chair
> Watching his looks, with kind and pensive air;
> Nor wife, nor sister she, nor is the name
> Nor kindred of this friendly pair the same;
> Yet so allied are they that few can feel
> Her constant, warm, unwearied, anxious zeal.
> Their years and woes, although they long have loved,
> Keep their good name and conduct unreproved;
> Thus life's small comforts they together share,
> And while life lingers, for the grave prepare.

The couple are Allen Booth and Judith. (We never learn her surname.) They met while young, fell in love, hoped to marry, but first Allen has to earn money, and a prospect opens of making his way in his kinsman's affairs in a 'western isle' – perhaps the West Indies. Allen sails away, promising to return, but never does. Or rather, when he finally makes it back to his 'native shore' forty years have passed and Allen is now 'A worn-out man, with withered limbs and lame'. As for Judith, after years of hoping for Allen to come back and marry her, she eventually yields to the suit of another man, who leaves her a widow by the time her former lover at last returns.

The story he has to tell is of some interest. It begins with his capture at sea by a Spanish vessel, transportation to somewhere in Central or South America, enslavement, where, 'hopeless ever to escape the land' he marries a Spanish girl, Isabel, by whom he has children though he is compelled to tell her the story of his lost love, and she 'wept in pity for the English maid'.

But after his Catholic captors discover that at heart he is still a Protestant, he is compelled to fly: 'Fly from all scenes, all objects of delight;/His wife, his children, weeping in his sight'. He then manages to get to the coast, boards a vessel, is impressed, fights for his country, dreams madly of his wife and family, of '"my lovely land,/See! There my dwelling"', is woken from these dreams, loses a limb in the Indian Ocean and eventually makes his way back to England: 'Anxious he felt on English earth to lie;/To view his native soil, and there to die.'

Sea-faring stories, tales of the sailor's return, are as old as Western literature itself. They exercise a particular hold on the English imagination and a thick strand of their braided narratives features lovers parted and, sometimes, though by no means always, restored to each other. Allen's return to Judith seems set up to join a long tradition which Dickens will later draw on in his account of the fraught love affair between Walter Gay and Florence Dombey. There is, though, a crucial difference. Dombey sends Walter, a mere office boy, to the West Indies. He will not allow his daughter to wed an upstart. But despite this, Walter eventually returns and marries Florence. Allen's return does not lead to marriage. On the contrary, he cannot shake off the memory of his marriage and his children. And so, when he tells Judith of his various misadventures, Crabbe notes that 'His were a medley of bewildering themes,/Sad as realities and wild as dreams.'

'Sad as realities and wild as dreams' is a key line, a key perception. Crabbe the realist focuses on Allen's troubled, unappeasable consciousness in order to dispel any hopes that he and Judith can become like Jesse Bourn and Colin Grey. Too much has happened in their lives for them to come together in any way other than as resigned, mutually suffering, yet compassionate friends. Allen dreams continually, and disturbingly, of the family he was forced to abandon.

So strong his eager fancy, he affrights
The faithful widow by its powerful flights,
For what disturbs him he aloud will tell,
And cry ''Tis she, my wife, my Isabel!
Where are my children?' – Judith grieves to hear
How the soul works in sorrows so severe.
Assiduous all his wishes to attend,
Deprived of much, he yet may boast a friend;
Watched by her care, in sleep his spirit takes
Its flight, and watchful finds her when he wakes.

It is intensely moving, this tender solicitude of Judith's for a man whose dreams are not of his former love for her but of his lost wife and family. Nor is there to be an affirmative ending to the tale. How can there be? Too much has happened in both their lives to allow for such a closure. And so, sat at his side, she watches over the sleeping Allen, notices the 'transient flushing of his cheeks', and knows that 'he is listening to the fancied noise/Of his own children, eager in their joys', – an eagerness that is both the children's and his. And sure enough, he 'wakes and cries – "My God! 'twas but a dream."'

And with that the Tale ends, as it must, on bafflement, sadness, and the only consolation available to both of them, that of her forbearance and his refuge in consolatory dreams, dreams from which he must awake to the comfortless reality of a wife and children forever lost to him.

VIII

One of the very greatest Tales, IV, 'Procrastination', has a similar starting point to 'The Parting Hour'. Here, the two young lovers are 'the prudent Dinah' and 'the kind Rupert'. As well as being a maid in waiting, Dinah is a kind of waiting maid to a rich aunt. Rupert follows his father's trade but neither he nor Dinah has the money to be able to marry. Yet, 'So long they now each other's thoughts had known/That nothing seemed exclusively their own'. At length, in their thirtieth year, a prospect opens, one that requires Rupert, like Allen, to take ship for 'in other clime', and though they are reluctant to be parted, the Aunt, rather like Jesse's rich protectress, promises that 'for this brief delay,/And Dinah's care, what I bequeath will pay'.

So Rupert takes ship and Dinah, left to dance attendance on her aunt, begins to find that the older woman's constant 'care' – one of the Tale's key words – is for money, one for which she begins to find an equal care. Or, as Crabbe puts it, a care in which she takes considerable pleasure: 'With lively joy those comforts she surveyed,/And love grew languid in the careful maid.' Prudence and care now meld to produce someone for whom material possessions count for more than her care for Rupert.

But Crabbe does not turn Dinah into a soulless materialist.

> Sometimes the past would on her mind intrude,
> And then a conflict full of care ensued.
> The thoughts of Rupert on her mind would press;
> His worth she knew, but doubted his success.

Here, 'care' is for other than money and goods and chattels. Dinah does still care for Rupert, hence the fact that thoughts would 'press', where the syntax, as elsewhere in the poem, brilliantly indicates the tortuous process by which Dinah's consciousness is, intermittently, at the mercy of her conscience. It is a moment which alerts us to the extraordinary subtlety with which Crabbe explores Dinah's mind.

It is undoubtedly a mind greatly affected by material considerations and her unruffled existence as companion to her aunt, and so well does Crabbe communicate these that the temptation, as so often, is simply to quote.

Month after month was passed, and all were spent
In quiet comfort and in rich content;
Miseries there were, and woes, the world around,
But these had not her pleasant dwelling found;
She knew that mothers grieved and widows wept,
And she was sorry, said her prayers, and slept.

Pure Crabbe, that last line, its laconicism part of his pointed armoury aimed at those whose impeccable behaviour, obedience to social decorum, goes with a steely egotism, an incuriosity which is rooted in, or which, for all Dinah's studious 'care', promotes a profound carelessness, a disregard for the lives of others.

And then comes a passage which has to be quoted in full and which is, I have no doubt, beyond compare in its attentive regard for Dinah's care of objects, her well-developed interest in all that can mark her out as a person of taste, someone of discernment, in short, a connoisseur, whose major concern is now with what money can buy.

Within that fair apartment guests might see
The comforts culled for wealth by vanity:
Around the room an Indian paper blazed,
With lively tint and figures boldly raised;
Silky and soft upon the floor below,
The elastic carpet rose with crimson glow;
All things around implied both cost and care,
What met the eye was elegant or rare:
Some curious trifles round the room were laid,
By Hope presented to the wealthy maid;
Within a costly case of varnished wood,
In level rows her polished volumes stood,
Shown as a favour to a chosen few,
To prove what beauty for a book could do;

A silver urn with curious work was fraught;
A silver lamp from Grecian pattern wrought;
Above her head, all gorgeous to behold,
A time-piece stood on feet of burnished gold;
A stag's-head crest adorned the pictured case,
Through the pure crystal shone the enamelled face,
And while on brilliants moved the hands of steel,
It clicked from prayer to prayer, from meal to meal.

Dinah, the woman of Taste, though not of ostentation. 'All things around *implied* both cost and care'. They don't, that is, shout it in your face. Dinah takes good 'care' to be discreet in her choice and arrangement of her possessions. Two points need to be made then about Crabbe's detailing of these. The first is that if you were to read the lines armed with a Salesroom catalogue of the time, you could work out, to within a few pounds, how much each item cost. The second is, that the same catalogue will reveal that these items make plain Dinah's shrewd understanding of fashion. You have only to compare the passage quoted earlier in which Crabbe describes the interior of Farmer Gwyn's 'Seat' to recognise how much more he is investing in his account of Dinah's possessions, and what they reveal about her.

For example, the Indian paper with its embossed figures ('boldly raised') has come from the Asian sub-continent. Walls thus papered not merely demonstrated the growing might of Empire, they were purchasable only by people with a good deal of money. They were also newly fashionable. For the walls of even fashionable houses of the period about which Crabbe is writing, and which we can safely assume is contemporaneous with the early years of the nineteenth century, when *Tales in Verse* was published, were typically either panelled or covered in plain papers, just as most floors were still bare or had their varnished boards dotted with rugs and mats. But Dinah has a carpet, and its 'crimson glow' suggests that it probably comes from Persia, which would have made it highly expensive.

Then, the books. As I have earlier noted, this was a time when book publishing was on the increase and much attention was paid to their presentation as well as how to house them in homes that lacked libraries, as most did. Varnished bookcases, the more superior kind with glass-fronted doors, were becoming a feature of many houses where there was money to spare, and inside them would be leather-bound books. Hence, Crabbe's pun on 'polished volumes'. Dinah's books are both gleaming with beeswax buffing and intended to display her good taste. And the 'level rows' show that she buys books in sets, as was the custom among those who could afford to purchase – say – the 'Ancients', Greek and Roman authors, to say nothing of such English masters as Bacon and Gibbon, whose works were issued as 'Complete' in several volumes. Dickens must have had Crabbe's lines about Dinah's books in mind when he came to describe Mr Dombey's library as housing books, 'precisely matched as to size, and drawn up, like soldiers, in their cold, hard, slippery uniforms', inside a locked bookcase, though, this being Dickens, the emphasis on the books' unwelcoming hardness has a metaphoric richness that not even Crabbe can equal.

He can, though, provide exact testimony to Dinah's awareness of the fashionable taste for the rococo. Hence, the silver urn and lamp, and hence, too, the time-piece with its stag's head and 'enamelled face,' of the kind that were on sale in the most fashionable show-rooms of the period. Dinah will have bought according to such taste, just as hopeful suitors will have presented her with 'curious trifles' – curios, in other words, such as those Gillray depicted in his mocking caricature of 1792, 'A Connoisseur examining a Cooper', in which a jowly gent – in fact George III – peers through a magnifying glass at a miniature portrait by the artist, Samuel Cooper (1609-72).

(The portrait is of Oliver Cromwell, a lovely ironic touch.) And, finally, Crabbe superbly indicates the sterility of Dinah's world of possession in that tart closing couplet about the clock which 'clicked from prayer to prayer, from meal to meal.' This is a time unrecompensed by event, a routine in which everything is reduced to an orderliness which permits no interruptions.

But then visiting friends mention how the 'young and gay' hide their wantonness and cover up their pasts, for 'what was once our pride is now our shame.'

> Dinah was musing, as her friends discoursed,
> When these last words a sudden entrance forced
> Upon her mind, and what was once her pride
> And now her shame some painful views supplied;
> Thoughts of the past within her bosom pressed,
> And there a change was felt, and was confessed.

Dinah's discomfort, her momentarily roused conscience, is made evident in syntax which breaks across the line-ending, disturbing the orderliness of the couplet form: 'these last words a sudden entrance forced/Upon her mind'. And now she is opened up to self-accusations which she is, for this moment at least, unable to resist. Thoughts of the past 'within her bosom *pressed,*/And there a change *was felt,* and *was confessed.*' (My italics.) Throughout the present book I have silently corrected the texts of the poems I have quoted from, usually by omitting commas strewn about the lines in a manner both unnecessary and hopelessly fussy; but here the comma between the two passive verbs is exactly right. It takes time for Dinah to move from the feeling that hurts her to acknowledgement of her past love for Rupert.

Crabbe does something very similar in Tale XIV, 'The Struggles of Conscience', about a young man called Fulham whose conscience becomes a kind of separate entity with whom he debates, or, more usually, which he finds himself having to confront in dialogue. At one point, after Conscience tells him reprovingly '"You wear a mask"', Fulham replies that '"If I have a view to serve myself, I serve the public too"', but when he is mocked by some religious zealots, 'it was felt within.'

Here is the same passive construction as is used of Dinah's reluctant awakening to thoughts of the past. Someone's words force their way into the protagonist's slumbering sub-conscious and so begin a kind of chain reaction, one that tracks from emotional disturbance to a fully intelligent acknowledgement of why the words bring pain. This awakening, unintentionally parodied in Holman Hunt's dire painting of 'The Awakening Conscience'(1852), in which a young prostitute is seen rising from a gentleman's lap, an expression of ardent but presumably un-orgasmic wonder on her face, is decisively Protestant. When the Anglican church assumed control in sixteenth-century England it replaced the public shows of Christian doctrine favoured by Roman Catholicism with private acceptance. Penitance, for example, became repentance. Dinah's awakening is a matter of emotional recognition, a perturbation, an *inner* sign, which then becomes one of intellectual acknowledgement.

Jane Austen does something more or less identical in showing the awakening to truth of her heroine, Emma, who near the end of the novel that bears her name suddenly realises why she doesn't want her friend Harriet Smith to marry Mr Knightley. It is because he must marry no-one but herself. 'A mind like hers, once opening to suspicion, made rapid progress; she touched, she admitted, she acknowledged the whole truth'. Here, though the verbs are active, the process is the same: from initial awakening ('opening'), through emotional response ('she touched') to intellectual awareness ('she acknowledged').

There is, though, a difference between the two. Emma's acknowledgement of the truth becomes permanent. With it, the novel can end. But 'Procrastination' doesn't end with Dinah's awakening to the truth of her feelings. She manages to shut her mind to her past love for Rupert. The former lover, now an aging man, eventually returns, his fortune unmade. 'In health declining as in mind distressed', Rupert is forced to accept parish charity. This is more than Dinah can bear. She sees him in the street and

> Some thoughts of pity raised by his distress,
> Some feeling touch of ancient tenderness,
> Religion, duty, urged the maid to speak
> In terms of kindness to a man so weak ...

But pride forbids. How then to behave? Simple. 'She crossed and passed him on the other side.' And *that* is where the poem ends. 'Procrastination' is one of the shortest of *Tales in Verse*. It is also a masterpiece.

IX

In a fuller account of the 1812 collection I would want to take note of the wit of Tale IX 'Arabella', in which Crabbe deftly, comically dissects the heroine's precise calculations as to whether she should marry and, if so, whom, calculations which are a delicious pastiche of what might be called rational good sense. 'On Captain Bligh her mind in balance hung – /Though valiant, modest, and reserved, though young;/Against these merits must defects be set – /Though poor, imprudent, and though proud, in debt ... ' I would want, too, to consider the magnanimous behaviour of the husband in Tale XVI, 'The Confidant', a tale concerned with a girl's seduction, the birth and death of her illegitimate baby, and consequent blackmail; and I would also want to say something about the sheer variety of human behaviour on show in other Tales such as XII, 'Squire Thomas; or, The Precipitate Choice', where a self-confident, not to say self-congratulatory young man becomes reluctantly aware of how poor a judge he is of others.

As it is, I hope I have done enough in the present chapter to make good my claim for the greatness of *Tales in Verse*. And at least I can end it by repeating that virtually all the great nineteenth-century novelists, from Jane Austen to Hardy, found in Crabbe, and especially in the work of 1812, themes, techniques, and an attentiveness to ordinary life in both its comic and darker aspects, which fed into much of their own finest work.

6

Tales of the Hall (1819)

I

Following the publication of *Tales in Verse* in 1812, and despite some reservations raised by critics which were considered in the previous chapter, Crabbe was now widely accepted as one of the major poets of the day. But he had little time to enjoy his critical success. The following year his wife died and he himself was taken seriously ill. Once he recovered he upped sticks and in 1814 moved to Trowbridge in Somerset. There, he briefly contracted an engagement to a Charlotte Ridout, a shadowy figure who soon disappeared and was never heard of again.

Anyone interested in Crabbe's life at this time should consult Neil Powell's biography. Here, it is enough to say that although the change of scene – including civil disturbances in 1816 – and visits to London took up some of his time, he was still occupied with writing poetry. *Tales of the Hall*, published in 1819 by Byron's publisher, John Murray, netted him £3,000, although he had to agree to tip in the copyright of all his previously published work before Murray handed him the money. £3,000 was a large sum, though not as great as Scott had been given for his earlier long poetic tales, *Marmion* (1808) and *The Lady of the Lake* (1810), let alone what Byron received for *Childe Harold*. (This first appeared in separate parts from 1812 to 1818, then in two-volume form in 1819, the year that *Don Juan* began to scandalise, entrance, and shake the world of poetry.) As well as being culturally acceptable to the widening circles of readers, poetry, it seems, was proving to be a profitable business for at least some writers and their publishers. And to read through Crabbe's letters during the period he was negotiating for publication by Murray, which required him to abandon Hatchard, his previous publisher, is to see that he was no slouch when it came to assessing his marketability. He was, and he knew he was, part of the success story of poetry at that time.

Various explanations have been offered for this success. One is that during the period of the Napoleonic wars getting the rags from which best-quality paper was made became increasingly difficult, because France, from which most of the rags came, was closed for trade to the British. Hence, poetry, which required less paper than novels, became more of an economic bargain for publishers. Although this explanation has often been given for poetry's advancement in the early nineteenth century, it seems both implausible – given the fact that many poetic works, including Crabbe's, were at least the length of most novels – and suspiciously Franco-phobe. (The French have plenty of rags to sell because the people there are so poor.) I am more persuaded by the argument that poetry was popular because as people began to develop libraries and therefore to vaunt their 'taste', so poetry was required to fill book shelves. The 'polished' volumes Dinah displays to her friends, given that they are presumably leather-bound, would, as I have already suggested, be mostly collections of the 'Classics' plus volumes of sermons, essays, and, of course, poetry. Poetry was literature. Prose fiction was not. Sarah Crabbe was among those many who did not approve of prose fiction, who thought it the devil's work, especially liable to appeal to, and therefore corrupt, young women – such as Farmer Moss' daughter – and therefore not to be given house-room.

Besides, poetry, if sufficiently well-produced, could be sold at a good asking price. People setting up or adding to libraries were not about to fill their shelves with ephemera, or at least with anything that looked cheap or shoddily produced. (The age of the paperback was the best part of a century ahead.) Leather-backed or fully bound volumes of poetry might be expensive, but as cultural artefacts that was part of their allure; for anyone wishing to demonstrate both wealth and good taste they were as desirable, even perhaps as necessary, as Persian carpets or rococo time-pieces. They didn't after all have to be read. It was quite enough for them to be on show, objects of admiration and proof of cultural attainment.

We are, of course, talking about a fairly small minority. In 1820 many people were barely literate, and comparatively few could afford to own books. Essential literature apart – most cottages possessed copies of the English bible and *The Pilgrim's Progress* – a large proportion of the population was virtually bookless. This was soon to change. The rise of the novel, which was at once cause and effect of increased literacy and the desire of publishers to provide books more cheaply than hitherto. And, as I have earlier indicated, most of the great nineteenth-century novelists learnt a thing or two from Crabbe. They, at least, had read him.

John Murray, who was certainly a shrewd publisher and therefore a hard-headed businessman, must have been reasonably confident that enough people would want to read, or anyway purchase, *Tales of the Hall*, as well as whatever earlier work of Crabbe's he might choose to re-publish now he owned the copyright, to justify the outlay of £3,000. There is ample evidence of the care he put into producing the collection of twenty-two tales that make up the handsome two-volume edition of 1819. This is not simply a matter of what now are called production values, though paper, half-leather binding, and type-face are all excellent. In addition, Murray took seriously his responsibilities as an editor. According to Gavin Edwards, in his Notes to the Penguin *George Crabbe: Selected Poems*, the new collection, *Tales of the Hall*, consists of 'twenty-two tales, selected by Crabbe from a series begun in 1814.'

I have no wish to quarrel with this, but my reading of the letters that Crabbe sent Murray while the work was being considered and after it had been accepted, makes pretty clear that Murray was active in shaping the book for publication. The title was his choice (Crabbe had proposed 'Forty Days'), he seems to have persuaded the poet to make a number of changes to the text, and there is little reason to doubt that he had a say in deciding which of the tales would constitute the final choice. 'Selection' was a joint decision of poet and publisher. In addition, Murray employed William Gifford, a well-known man of letters, to act as copy editor and proof-reader, a task which Gifford, if Crabbe's letters are anything to go by, seems to have undertaken with due zeal and care. 'I am much indebted to Mr Gifford,' Crabbe tells Murray in March, 1819, '& heartily wish I had his Judgement to assist me in the parts more particularly where I find my own deficient. I hope the lines are varied for the better,' he adds, which indicates that Gifford has succeeded in getting him to reconsider and re-write lines the copy-editor found unsatisfactory.

II

The idea for the collection seems to have come to Crabbe at about the time he moved to Trowbridge. In 1814, he tentatively gave a working title of 'Remembrances' to tales which would be spoken by two brothers, turn and turn-about. This framing device provided the chance for alternative points of view, for the brothers – half-brothers in fact – meet at the Hall where they had last seen each other in infancy. Now, past middle-age, there are marked differences between them. George, a moderate Tory who has done well out of life, tells Richard, less successful, a one-time (faintly) radical Whig, about his own past successes, about people he has met, about friends; and Richard does likewise. The brothers are not Sir Roger de Coverley and Sir Andrew Freeport *redivivus*, but the opposing points of view, which had served Addison well a hundred years earlier in the more polemical pages of *The Spectator*, are usefully recruited for Crabbe's lengthy narrative.

Tales of the Hall got off to a good start. A year after first publication it was into its third edition and in the same year Murray brought out what Crabbe, in a letter to his publisher, called 'the uniform Edition of all the Poems, Tales, Etc', which appeared in seven volumes. Moreover, the critical reception was, if not adulatory, undoubtedly enthusiastic. 'Burns, Wordsworth, and Crabbe, are the three poets who, in our days, have most successfully sought the subjects and scenes of their inspiration in the character and life of the People.' So begins the review by John Wilson in *Blackwood's Edinburgh Review*, and Wilson, or 'Christopher North' to use his pseudonym, goes on to say that Crabbe is 'the most original and vivid painter of the vast varieties of common life, that England has ever produced.' Moreover, the poet 'lays bare, with an unshrinking hand, the very arteries of the heart ... Of all men of the age, he is the best portrait-painter. He is never contented with a single flowing sketch of a character – they must all be drawn full-length – to the very life – and with their most minute and characteristic features, even of dress and manners.' Crabbe is both surgeon and, as it were, dispassionate analyst of the people he anatomises.

This praise finds its counterpart, though with something of a twist, in Francis Jeffrey's lengthy essay for the *Edinburgh Review*. Jeffrey, an unabashed admirer, notes that Crabbe's heart 'is always open to pity, and all the milder emotions', but that he has little or nothing to say about raptures and ecstasies. Read one way, this is an endorsement of Crabbe's anti-romantic muse, of a realism that rejects the cult of un- or other-worldly heroics. This is the poet as Mr Austen.

But read another, it is as if Jeffrey secretly laments how very level Crabbe's gaze always is. This is as we should expect. Crabbe is not a poet to be carried away by emotional highs and lows. He registers them, but he doesn't endorse them. He is not, as I have already noted, a tragic poet, and love is often entwined with tragedy. (Of the epigraphs attached to the XXI *Tales in Verse* only two come from *Othello*, none at all from *Romeo and Juliet*.) But the advantage of the level gaze is that it is not liable to distortion, and Jeffrey recognises this when he praises the poet for refusing to meddle with 'the delicate distresses and noble fires of the heroes and heroines of tragic and epic fable.' Instead, the poet

> may generally be detected indulging in a lurking sneer at the pomp and vanity of all such superfine imaginations – and turning to draw men in their true postures and dimensions, and with all the imperfections that belong to their condition: – the prosperous and happy overshadowed with passing clouds of *ennui*, and disturbed with little flaws of bad humour and discontent – the great and wise beset at times with strange weaknesses and meannesses and paltry vexations – and even the most virtuous and enlightened falling far below the standard of poetical perfection – and stooping every now and then to paltry jealousies and prejudices – or sinking into shabby sensualities, – or meditating on their own excellence and importance, with a ludicrous and lamentable anxiety. (CH, p. 232)

'Sneer' may seem to suggest that Jeffrey thinks Crabbe unduly dismissive of the superfine imagination, but Johnson gave as one of the word's definitions 'to show contempt', and in this sense 'sneer' isn't like Ozymandias' 'sneer of cold command', because it doesn't imply the dismissive condescension of superior power or class assumptions of entitlement. (Interestingly, Shelley's great sonnet was being written at exactly the same time as Jeffrey's review was published.)

I have quoted Jeffrey's remarks at some length, not only because they provide such an excellent summing-up of many of Crabbe's virtues, but because they identify a quality especially to be found in *Tales of the Hall*. Not always, not even often, but, where it occurs, anticipatory of the work of Henry James.

III

A glance at the London Journal Crabbe kept in 1817 suggests, however, comparison with another and altogether inferior nineteenth-century novelist. On 5 July 1817, he notes 'My thirty lines done; but not well, I fear: thirty daily is self-engagement.' Three days later, he records, 'Thirty lines to-day; but not yesterday: must work up.' And then, on 15 July, 'Wrote some lines in the solitude of Somerset House, not fifty yards from the Thames on one side, and the Strand on the other; but as quiet as the sands of Arabia.' Whether Crabbe set himself this 'drudging', to use Dryden's word, all the time he was at work compiling what would become *Tales of the Hall*, I don't know, though I doubt it. But there is something Trollopian in this banausic determination to do his daily quota, something, too, reminiscent of Johnson's 'Sir any man may write if he will set himself doggedly to do it.' This goes with another of Johnson's dicta: 'Nobody but a fool ever wrote but for money.'

There is no evidence that Crabbe was in need of money. But the collection of 1819 undoubtedly suffers from some pretty humdrum writing. Dogged is the word. It is as though Crabbe grits his teeth and forces himself to get on with what, for all can be thought to the contrary, he saw as an uncongenial task.

Not so much Pope in worsted stockings, perhaps, as the man in the grey suit.

It may be an awareness of this which caused the reviewer in the *Christian Observer* to complain that Crabbe is incapable of the epic. 'Well, of course, he is.' Jeffrey's growl of contemptuous dismissal is within earshot. But in an admittedly clumsy way the reviewer is, I suspect, trying to put his finger on what seems to be lacking from the 1819 collection. There is too much, he says, 'of that "sermo pedestris" which he seems to make the grand characteristic of all his writings.' (CH, p. 256-7) Hence, Crabbe's openings, which are 'most ordinarily in that low and *chatty* sort of language.' (Reviewer's italics.) They are not warmed by a true regard. Crabbe is going through the motions.

The *Monthly Review* is even more severe. The concision and finished excellence of Crabbe's earlier work has by and large gone, we are told, 'while in the great majority of rhymes he cares little for cadence and less for expression, and, above all his other faults, offends by a tautology that is equally feeble and unpoetical.' (CH, p. 273). The *Eclectic Review* is a good deal more complimentary, though the same criticism surfaces when the reviewer comments on Crabbe's willingness to make life hard for the reader: 'we felt ourselves continually to stand in need of … inducement in persevering through Mr Crabbe's volumes; so often was the pleasure he is always capable of affording, suspended by the positively disagreeable qualities of the narration, or the worse than ill-chosen nature of his subject.' (CH, p. 285). We've been here before. The level gaze takes in much that the poet's eye ought to soar above. What is new, I think, is a feeling that Crabbe himself is offering nothing new, that he's re-cycling old material.

But then, and as though making amends for what he decides was his carking tone, the reviewer concludes by saying that *Tales of the Hall* exhibits 'no marks of decay or exhaustion of faculty.' And though Crabbe's manner is 'too cool, too dry', for even his admirers to take as a model, the poems that make up the two volumes could only have been written by someone who has 'lived long, and seen much of life, in order to have acquired that treasure of good and evil knowledge from which Mr Crabbe draws his seemingly inexhaustible materials.' (CH. p. 289).

Evil? The word seems too large for Crabbe and surely flies in the face of Jeffrey's praise for the poet's refusal to indulge himself in either the heroic or the tragic extremes of human existence. But if 'regulated hatred' is a term that applies to Jane Austen, so, I think, an awareness and exploration of evil is something that is there in Crabbe. Peter Grimes is evil. He has the power to do harm to people subservient to him and he chooses to do it. He murders because he *can*. That was one of the things Dickens understood about Crabbe when he fashioned characters such as Bill Sikes and Orlick. But evil can occur in subtler, less openly stated ways, as it does, I suggest in 'The Mother' where egotism requires a denial of the separate reality of another person – in this case, as we have seen, Dorothea's own daughter. Egotism always is like this, of course. Other people exist merely to serve the egotist's purpose. After Dickens, whose novels are full of such purposive evil, and making due allowance for the presentation of Grandcourt in George Eliot's *Daniel Deronda*, Henry James is the great master when it comes to exploring the destructive power of egotism. But Crabbe anticipates them both. Egotism, even when less blatant, more teasingly problematic, is at the heart of one of the *Tales of the Hall* which seems to me to take Crabbe into deeper territory than he had ever before explored.

IV

This may seem contentious and the remark ought to be qualified at least to the extent that, quite apart from 'The Mother', a tale such as 'Procrastination' explores with great subtlety the devious ways in which the human psyche can adjust itself to accept and so justify the intolerable. Dinah's behaviour toward her erstwhile lover, Rupert, her rejection of him, not by repudiating but by ignoring him, is as plausible as it is shocking. Her act of choosing to pass him by 'on the other side' may hint at a guilty conscience; but it may equally tell us that she has successfully killed those feelings of guilt to which, earlier in the tale, we had been made privy. We can't be sure, because at the end of the tale we are outside Dinah, watching her but not given her thoughts; we can't therefore be entirely confident how to interpret her action. She behaves badly, but because we can't know her mind we can't do more than say that her behaviour is reprehensibly cold-hearted, and that what she does – and doesn't do – is at best obtuse and uncaring.

But in 'Delay Has Danger,' Book XIII of *Tales of the Hall*, we know all that is going on in the mind of the tale's protagonist, Henry. And though it may seem grandiloquent to suggest that what he does is evil, the fact remains that he wrecks three lives through his actions. Or, as they may seem, inactions. For though the title 'Delay Has Danger' may seem to apply to his lingering for longer than he should apart from Cecilia, the young woman to whom he is betrothed, he delays his return because of his recognition, one which rouses a certain languid vanity, that he seems to be favoured by another young woman called Fanny, whose submissive appeal to him is both flattering and, it turns out, dangerous in ways he had not accounted for.

Brother Richard is the brother who starts the tale off, prompted, he tells George, by memories of a town called Silford, in a part of the country which he calls

... a lovely place, and at the side
Rises a mountain-rock in rugged pride;
And in that rock are shapes of shells, and forms
Of creatures in old worlds, of nameless worms,
Whose generations lived and died ere man,
A worm of other class, to crawl began.

Gavin Edwards has a lengthy note about these lines, pointing out not only that Raymond Williams includes Crabbe's use of 'class' in his seminal work *Keywords*, but that 'Fanny and Richard stand alone in the society of an aristocratic household, on a "border land" between classes, families, and stages in the life-cycle. In this study of social stratification Crabbe links social and natural-historical meanings of the word "class"'. (p. 502.)

This is helpful, although I am less convinced by Edwards' suggestion that at the beginning of the poem, when Richard rides to 'Farley Grange', Crabbe intends a bow toward his own friend, Colonel Houlton, who lived at Farleigh Castle, Somerset, not far from Trowbridge. Silford and its surroundings are, it seems to me, described in a manner suggestive of the Derbyshire Peak District, whose hills are remarkable for the number of fossils preserved in its limestone rock. It was the discovery and attempted classification of these which in the period Crabbe was writing did much to topple the conventional view of the world's age and of its 'birth' in c. 4,000 BC. And, without wishing to push speculation too far, it seems proper to note that Erasmus Darwin, whose *Zoonomia* (1794) did much to open up arguments about evolution, lived until his death in 1802 in Derbyshire. It was there that he wrote the following passage which appears as part of the Conclusion to *Zoonomia*: 'Would it be too bold to imagine that, in the great length of time since the world began to exist, perhaps millions of years before the commencement of the history of mankind,

– would it be too bold to imagine that all warm-blooded animals have arisen from one living filament … ' Human beings may be worms of 'other class' but, Crabbe says, they are still worms, and in so saying he echoes Darwin. And this is further echoed when George tells brother Richard at one point in the Tale that, '"man has reptile-pride/That often rises when his fears subside"'.

Moreover, although the tale certainly takes note of, and uses the fact of, 'social stratification' to reveal the harmful effect liable to follow from attempts to cross the 'border-land' from one class to another, to leave it at that would be seriously to underrate its originality. 'Delay Has Danger' undoubtedly takes a conservative view of class' supposedly immutable boundaries, but the tale isn't a grimmer version of Harriet Smith's vain wish to aspire to marriage with Mr Knightly before sensibly accepting to become the wife of farmer Martin. Yes, in the story the brothers bat about between themselves, Henry ends up by losing his original love, the 'tall, fair, lovely lady', Cecilia, and instead is by his own inanition drawn into a disastrous marriage with Fanny, who belongs, as it were 'below stairs'. But what interests Crabbe is how exactly this comes about. Richard has heard the story, but, he tells George, '"Of this affair I have a clouded view"', to which his brother replies that although he himself '"had the story from the injured side"', he is confident he understands all that happened, and why. '"Frail was the hero of my tale,"' he says, '"but still/Was rather drawn by accident than will"', adding that '"Some without meaning into guilt advance,/From want of guard, from vanity, from chance"'.

Neither brother is to be thought of as an unreliable narrator. George quite certainly tells the tale as he sees it, and although he relies on Cecilia's version of events, she relates what she knows to him only after '"resentment and regret were gone,/And pity (shaded by contempt) came on."' Nevertheless, we realise that, given this convoluted mode of story-telling,

George has to invent some moments he couldn't have witnessed, any more than could Cecilia, just as he has to guess at conversations which he was in no position to overhear. He doesn't say this, but then he doesn't need to. Once he says to Richard – he is talking of the way he imagines Henry pressed his suit with Cecilia – '"Let us suppose with many a sigh there came/The declaration of the deathless flame"', we know we have to accept at face value his attempt to present the narrative as transpicuously as he can, but this still leaves us free to judge what is going on in a way that departs from his good-natured interpretation. In other words, Crabbe is here developing a narrative mode which will become a major structural device in prose fiction. 'Delay Has Danger' is a tale pieced together by those who are outsiders and who have to rely on the testimony of others to get at the truth.

George is a decent, bluff, squirearchical figure, the sort often called 'Fieldingesque'. Reporting on what he imagines to be Cecilia's initial rebuff of Henry, he says, '"Ladies, like towns besieged, for honour's sake,/Will some defence or its appearance make"'; but eventually '"each the other's valiant acts approve,/And twine their laurels in a wreath of love."' Henry and Cecilia, we can infer, are well-matched, like Beatrice and Benedick, or, of course, like Sybil and Josiah.

But, in a move conventional enough in love stories, and one Crabbe had earlier used in, for example, 'The Parting Hour', and 'Jesse and Colin', true love is put to the test when Henry is ordered by his father to make a journey to 'our patron'. '"Cecilia liked it not; she had, in truth,/No mind to part from her enamoured youth."' But fathers must be obeyed and although Cecilia fears that Henry's journey may lead to disaster – which she imagines as a hunting accident or her lover dying in a duel – '"Prudence answered, 'Is not every maid/With equal cause for him she loves afraid?'/And from her guarded mind Cecilia threw/The groundless terrors that will love pursue."'

Moreover:

> Firm in herself, she doubted not the truth
> Of him, the chosen, the selected youth;
> Trust of herself a trust in him supplied,
> And she believed him faithful, though untried;
> On her he might depend, in him she would confide.

This is a marriage of true minds, or so Cecilia believes. And she goes on believing though a month passes and, notwithstanding Henry's having named to her a day for his return, '"still my lord was kind, and Henry still must stay:/His father's words to him were words of fate – /'Wait, 'tis your duty; 'tis my pleasure, wait!'"'

Well, fathers are tyrants, as Emma Woodhouse can't bring herself to admit; and disobeying them can bring not merely contumely down on you but loss of fortune and estate. Besides, Henry decides that in his lonely sojourn, having the place to himself in his walks and in '"those forsaken rooms, in that immense saloon"' he can at least read Cecilia's letters and write his to her. '"'Here none approach,' said he, 'to interfere,/But I can think of my Cecilia here!'"'

But then his peace is disturbed by the unexpected coming of

> ... a mild and blue-eyed lass –
> It was the work of accident, no doubt,
> The cause unknown – we say, 'as things fall out'; –
> The damsel entered there, in wandering round about:
> At first she saw not Henry; and she ran,
> As from a ghost, when she beheld a man.

George's way of telling the story is hesitant, fussy, almost, and conventional. We never know whether the girl's interruption of Henry's solitude was an accident or whether it was planned. And if it *was* planned, then by whom? The girl herself or her parents? Because when these belatedly appear, it is to tell Henry that they have been watching how the young man's affection for the girl has grown, as has hers for him, to the point where they take for granted the inevitability of their marrying.

But before we come to that moment, Crabbe provides evidence in plenty of how Henry's susceptibilities are flattered by Fanny's attention. Initially silent, always timid, her behaviour implies, so he comes to believe, admiration, even love of him. It makes him unusually eloquent, a man of feeling who, in speaking of the scene before them in one walk where they unexpectedly – is it? – meet, asks her whether she enjoys the view as much as he does: '"Something it has that words will not express,/But rather hide, and make the enjoyment less: /'Tis what our souls conceive, 'tis what our hearts confess.'"'

We can't find words adequate to convey our sense of the landscape, he is saying, but he could as well be talking about their feelings for each other. And what we now must sense is how he is leading her on, not consciously, but because it's so delightful to have this girl pay him such rapt attention. Her words, when they come, flatter him as much as, if not more than, the way she looks at him. She must not be seen with him, she says, because she is afraid:

> 'Not, sir, of you; your goodness I can trust,
> But folks are so censorious and unjust,
> They make no difference, they pay no regard
> To our true meaning, which is very hard
> And very cruel; great the pain it cost
> To lose such pleasure, but it must be lost:
> Did people know how free the thought of ill
> One's meaning is, their malice would be still.'

171

At this she wept; at least a glittering gem
Shone in each eye, and there was fire in them,
For as they fell, the sparkles at his feet,
He felt emotions very warm and sweet …

Our lover then believed he must not seem
Cold to the maid who gave him her esteem;
Not manly, this; Cecilia had his heart,
But it was lawful with his time to part …

Who is fooling who? We can't know, but we can be certain she acts as 'the flame that waked his vanity'. And how deftly Crabbe shows Henry sophisticating his reasons for continuing to see – and be flattered by – someone to whom he convinces himself he must behave in a 'manly' way, especially as such behaviour is 'lawful'.

The outcome of the relationship, though, given that nothing direct is said on either side, 'relationship' hardly seems the proper word, is that Henry is burnt by getting too close to the flame. Cecilia sends letters in which she mingles disquiet at what she has heard of his dallying with a demand that he return to her. (The words dallying, delay, and dalliance – 'talk, amorous toying' – seem to elide into each other.) Reason urges the young man to do as Cecilia says: "'Uneasy, anxious, filled with self-reproof,/He now resolved to quit his patron's roof.'" But "'then again his vacillating mind/To stay resolved'". The syntax brilliantly implies that Henry is helplessly led by reason – 'his mind' – to do what reason tells him he shouldn't. It isn't *his* fault. And so when he writes to Cecilia he dares to rebuke her, presumably for her lack of trust in him.

And then comes the fateful meeting with Fanny's adoptive parents. Fanny and Henry are taking "'their usual ramble'" when they encounter the steward, a rather grand, imposing figure with "'News in his look, and gladness in his face.'" "'My esteemed young man,'" he calls Henry, before telling him he knows that the youth and Fanny must wish to marry. Useless for Henry to try to explain himself, because the steward claims he has money to supply their wants, and he then leaves, allowing his wife to tell Henry that her husband is not a man to be thwarted, that she herself has made Fanny confess her love for Henry, that the two parents have told the Lord of the place, Henry's patron, about the couple, who has blessed the union, and that she has some letters for him, written in a female hand, which must be from a sister, because Henry would not be a deceiver, which allows her to conclude that his love for Fanny must be pure and whole: "'Now mind that none with her divide your heart,/For she would die ere lose the smallest part.'"

The twists in the plotting by which Henry becomes trapped are managed with devilish subtlety and in truth we never really know whether his downfall – his commitment to Fanny, bewildered, reluctant, resented, but irrevocable – was planned from the outset, and if so by whom – the girl, her parents, or all three? – or whether it simply happened. But he is caught, and can't wriggle free. This is narrative art which serves a most subtle psychological purpose, and I would say that Crabbe's probing at the desperate consequences that can come from Henry's kind of thoughtless and seemingly harmless, inconsequential vanity is taken up by George Eliot in *Adam Bede*. For in that early novel, the seduction of the thoughtless Hetty Sorrel by the young, vain, but casually well-meaning young squire, Arthur Donnithorne, proves to be an act with ineluctable and disastrous consequences.

George Eliot read Crabbe. I have no evidence to suggest that Henry James also read him. Nevertheless, it is instructive in this context to mention James' early masterpiece, *Washington Square*, which has at its heart the exploitative relationship between a fortune hunter, Morris Townsend, and Catherine

Sloper, the plain-looking young woman he lays siege to, and then cries off from when her father reveals that should she marry Townsend he won't get a penny of her fortune. It isn't the similarity of outer narrative that interests me here so much as the way James, like Crabbe and Eliot before him, explores the damage done by false emotional claims, and all three are, I think, alert to the reality of evil which comes from their male protagonists' readiness to make use of others in order to gain their own ends. To be sure, Eliot's meliorist view of the human heart leads her to suggest that self-knowledge can and will bring about a better way of ordering relationships. Crabbe and James would be far more likely than her to nod with a grim smile of approval at that couplet of Landor's about how 'Triumphant Demons stand, and Angels start,/To see the abysses of the human heart', though both would feel that the abysses are hidden from those whose hearts bear witness to them.

Henry is scarcely aware of the vanity that leads him on, and at moments when he *does* become troublingly aware of intruding into what Yeats, in a different context, called 'the labyrinth of another's being', he tries to shrug off or elude his own conscience. But, as George Eliot says, 'Our deeds determine us as much as we determine our deeds.' Arthur Donnithorne, in some ways a replication of Henry, has 'a sort of implicit confidence in him that he was really such a good fellow at bottom, Providence would not treat him harshly', but, as Mrs Poyser, the dealer in home truths in *Adam Bede* says, 'there are some things that can't be made up for', and Henry's fate is the cost of his involvement with Fanny.

The pair marry, and Fanny turns out to be as shallow as he had, we sense, known her to be: '"Jealous and tender, conscious of defects,/She merits little, yet she much expects"'. At the end of the poem Henry reflects:

Her beauty vanished, what for me remains?
The eternal clicking of the galling chains:
Her person truly I may think my own,
Seen without pleasure, without triumph shown:
Doleful she sits, her children at her knees,
And gives up all her feeble powers to please;
Whom I, unmoved, or moved with scorn, behold,
Melting as ice, as vapid and as cold.

Crabbe ruthlessly undermines the introspective, brooding quality of Henry's separateness from his wife and family, testified to in his reference to 'her' children, as though he has no part in their lives. Self-pity and wounded vanity are interwoven into Henry's thoughts. He can't even show his wife off with 'triumph' as a treasured possession. What for *me* remains. No thought of what remains for her.

V

Crabbe's acute anatomising of the workings of the psyche, here, of the implications and consequences of egotism, is an essential part of his greatness. In a characteristic passage toward the end of 'Delay Has Danger,' when Henry realises he is to be trapped into a loveless marriage, he rises early and looks

… with many a sigh
On the red light that filled the eastern sky;
Oft had he stood before, alert and gay,
To hail the glories of the new-born day;
But now dejected, languid, listless, low,
He saw the wind upon the water blow,
And the cold stream curled onward as the gale
From the pine-hill blew harshly down the dale;

On the right side the youth a wood surveyed,
With all its dark intensity of shade;
Where the rough wind alone was heard to move,
In this, the pause of nature and of love,
When now the young are reared, and when the old,
Lost to the tie grow negligent and cold –
Far to the left he saw the huts of men,
Half hid in mist that hung upon the fen;
Before him swallows, gathering for the sea,
Took their short flights, and twittered on the lea;
And near the bean-sheaf stood, the harvest done,
And slowly blackened in the sickly sun;
All these were sad in nature, or they took
Sadness from him, the likeness of his look,
And of his mind – he pondered for a while,
Then met his Fanny with a borrowed smile.

We have been here before. The *tour-de-force* account of Peter Grimes' self-communing on the mud flats shows what Crabbe can do in rendering the introversions of the mind as it receives and interprets according to its own subjective mood the outer landscape.

Equally remarkable, though exploited for comic purpose, there are the 'interpreted' landscapes of 'The Lover's Journey', number X of the 1812 *Tales*. Crabbe opens this with the memorable statement that 'It is the Soul that sees; the outward eyes/Present the object, but the Mind descries;/And thence delight, disgust, or cool indifference rise'. And elaborating on this, he adds:

When minds are joyful, then we look around,
And what is seen is all on fairy ground;
Again they sicken, and on every view
Cast their own dull and melancholy hue;

Or, if absorbed by their peculiar cares,
The vacant eye on viewless matter glares;
Our feelings still upon our views attend,
And their own natures to the objects lend;
Sorrow and joy are in their influence sure,
Long as the passion reigns the effects endure ...

A passage such as this, endlessly replicated in Crabbe's work, not merely reminds us of Dryden in its capacity for 'argufying', but shows that Crabbe is often Dryden's equal in what was once called the earlier poet's 'ratiocination.'

But there is a more particular reason for noting the lines. 'The vacant eye' inevitably recalls the lines in 'I Wandered Lonely As A Cloud', where Wordsworth records how 'When often on my couch I lie/In vacant or in pensive mood/[the Daffodils] flash upon my inward eye.' For Wordsworth memory has an agency, a power to start up unaided by conscious decision, by what we might call taking thought. Emptied out, vacant, his mind or inner eye is filled with the vision of the daffodils and the delight of their dancing. There is, in other words, a mysterious transaction between outer and inner worlds. Crabbe, on the other hand, is more tentative about the relationship of the two worlds. 'All these were sad in nature, or they took/Sadness from him ... '

In 'The Lover's Journey' John, who styles himself Orlando, journeys on horse-back to see Susan (or 'Laura' as he dubs her in honour of Petrarch). As he travels on, he transforms outer nature into a blessed landscape. He rides across 'a barren heath beside the coast' but sees and smells delight: what he calls 'gay ling, with all its purple flowers/ ... This green-fringed cup-moss has a scarlet tip/That yields to nothing but my Laura's lip'; and so on. Crabbe adds a long prose note in which, among much else, he remarks that 'The ditches of a Fen so near the ocean are lined with irregular patches of a coarse and stained

Laver; a muddy sediment rests on the Horse-tail and other perennial herbs … An effluvia strong and peculiar, half-saline, half-putrid, which would be considered by most people as offensive, and by some as dangerous; but there are others to whom the singularity of taste or association of ideas has rendered it agreeable and pleasant.'

The mention of 'association of ideas' is a reference to David Hartley (1707-1757), that law-giver for the latter part of the eighteenth century on the mind and the nature of perception. Hartley, as I have earlier noted, was a powerful influence on the young Coleridge, who named his first son after the philosopher, and though he came to reject as 'mechanical' Hartley's associationism, the doctrine, if it may be so called, retained a powerful influence on habits of thought during the period Crabbe was writing. I doubt that Crabbe's reference is much more than casual or opportunistic. But quite apart from his own strong interest in the flora of what Gavin Edwards has called borderland, and the opportunity his tale gives him to indulge this, he can exploit for comic effect the way 'Orlando' chooses to transform the most unpropitious landscape by an eye which in this instance is far from vacant.

But then he reaches his destination, finds 'Laura' has gone to visit a friend, and, riding in sullen pursuit, passes through a fine, rich, well-farmed landscape, complaining of its dullness which he associates with exploitation and profit-and-loss. In fact, in many ways he 'reads' this landscape as more than two centuries later John Berger 'reads' Gainsborough's portrait of a smiling Mr and Mrs Andrews in front of well-tilled fields. Why are they smiling? Because they own it all.

As for Orlando:

> 'These deep fat meadows I detest; it shocks
> One's feelings there to see the grazing ox; –
> For slaughter fatted, as a lady's smile

Rejoices man and means his death the while.
Lo! Now the sons of labour, every day
Employed in toil, and vexed in every way;
Theirs is but mirth assumed, and they conceal,
In their affected joys, the ills they feel;
I hate these long green lanes, there's nothing seen
In this vile country but eternal green;
Woods! waters! Meadows! Will they never end!
'Tis a vile prospect: – Gone to see a friend!'

Crabbe brings us back to the comic aspect of all this at the end of the verse paragraph. And yet the young man's outrage at what the well-tended landscapes of enclosure portend has its justification. The sons of labour *are* vexed by the demands of the farmers who have control over their lives, and from whom they must conceal their ills, resentment at poor wages and rotten living conditions, in phony displays of 'joys' – gratitude for being granted back-breaking employment on the land they no longer own. 'Vexed' now means not much more than 'irritated', but Johnson gives the meaning of the verb 'vex' as: 'to plague, torment, harass', a use which survives in John Crowe Ransom's perfect poem, 'Bells For John Whiteside's Daughter', where the mourners gathering for the little girl's funeral are 'vexed by her brown study'. This is how Crabbe must be using the word. In other words, as there are those for whom the barren, inhospitable heath has its genuine pleasures, so the rich landscape can prompt decidedly uneasy thoughts about what its riches imply.

To repeat, 'The Lover's Tale' is a comic narrative, and as he accompanies his beloved 'Laura' back to her lodging, 'Orlando' has no time to observe the landscape at all: 'The mind was filled, was happy, and the eye/Roved o'er the fleeting views that but appeared to die.' Later, when he has left Laura and is on his own, he is similarly unengaged by a landscape now viewed by 'the vacant eye [which] Wandered o'er viewless scenes, that but appeared to die.' For Crabbe, a vacant eye is incapable of absorbing outer nature. Such absorption, such attraction to particular scenes and the interpretive process involved in how they are viewed, requires an active, to-fro connection between viewer and what is viewed.

This is the import of the scene Henry views in 'Delay Has Danger'. Henry's appalled awakening to the fact that he has ruined his own life, and perhaps that of another, is confirmed by the bleakness of a landscape in which he isolates those features that reinforce, or that he intuits as imposing on him, his realisation that he has wasted his prospects. This is as close as he comes to understanding the dark horror of what he has wrought. Evil: the word may seem too strong to apply to his shallow vanity and the exploitation of Fanny's feelings, especially as it seems entirely possible that she has exploited *him*, and that, even if this is not so, her adoptive parents have manipulated the flirtation to their own ends. To repeat, that we can't be sure of any of this is due to the great subtlety with which Crabbe handles the narrative. But what we can be sure of is Henry's collusion in his own 'waste'.

Of course, he doesn't *mean* this to happen. We are throughout the tale made aware of Henry's obtuse inability to take responsibility for his actions. Delay, dalliance, deferral, they are at the core of his being. Hence, the lines where a dull passiviness operates as he is brought to register how in the wood, "'With all its dark intensity of shade'" – that familiar trope of a disordered world, – "'the rough wind alone was heard to move'". Five years before the publication of *Tales of the Hall*, the first English translation of *The Divine Comedy*, Henry Cary's *The Vision of Hell, Purgatory, and Paradise, by Dante Alighieri* made its appearance. It began with what was to become one of the most famous of all openings in English poetry, endlessly echoed and adapted by later poets: 'In the midway of this our mortal life,/I found me in a gloomy wood, astray/Gone from the path direct.'

I don't know whether Crabbe read Cary's translation. He is likely to have done so, although the rough wind from the wood which tells Henry how far he is astray in his own life is markedly different from the one that wakes Dante to acknowledgement of his predicament. For Henry there is no awakening, except to dull, enervate acceptance. '"Where the rough wind alone was heard to move"'. As the passive verb indicates, Henry lacks the will or wit to take responsibility for his own life. It's as though he is the hapless listener to a truth that obtrudes on his consciousness, carrying the news that in '"this pause of nature and of love"' life is a matter of dull routine, where '"the young are reared"' and '"the old,/Lost to the tie, grow negligent and cold."' The shudder these lines induce are to my mind similar to the great moment in *Dombey and Son* where the aged Mrs Skewton, who has wrecked her own and her daughter's lives, is wheeled down to the shore at Brighton and can see only 'a broad stretch of desolation between earth and heaven.'

VI

I have chosen to concentrate my discussion of *Tales of the Hall* on 'Delay Has Danger' because its greatness is, it seems to me, so apparent, and yet has rarely been acknowledged. I hope, however, the attention I have lavished on this one tale won't be taken to imply that there are no other tales worth reading in the collection of 1819, because, as its earlier reviewers noted, there are. None of these reviewers, though, no matter how favourable they are, has much to say about the 'framing' Crabbe uses to set the tales in motion. To be sure, most, if not all, commentators make mention of it. The device of having the two half-brothers meet and discuss their very different lives is after all a neat gimmick, an ingenious contrivance to enable the telling of a wide variety of tales. Commentators remark on this, but that is as far as they go.

But the fact is that from the outset of his career, Crabbe had been trying different ways of producing narrative poems. At first, he had presented himself, poet and teller of tales, as a kind of overseer of country customs, mores, institutions. The poet as natural historian of rural and semi-urban life. Hence, *The Library, The Village, The Newspaper*, and, after that a twenty-two-year break during which he had written novels, *The Parish Register* and *The Borough*.

The 1812 collection, *Tales in Verse*, is, though, different. Crabbe is now unashamedly writing fiction. He isn't studying the occupants of any one place in particular. The Tales he has to tell are set in different places, concern a wide range of people, deal in a variety of circumstances and occurrences. As I have repeatedly noted in this monograph, Crabbe is interested in all the things that we take to be the characteristic features of novels in the great realistic tradition: the outer life of dress, of habitat, of domestic circumstance, and of how to 'read' character through possessions and habits; the use of conversation to reveal character, the study of people's innermost lives as shown in speech and behaviour. *Tales of the Hall* isn't a novel in verse, of the kind we find in Browning and Tennyson. But it opens up territory which they will be able to enter.

And there is a further point to make here. The long narrative poem had become enormously popular in the late years of the eighteenth century, and continued to be so all the while Crabbe was writing. Many of the settings for these narratives were exotic. They were set in foreign parts – Landor's 1798 poem, *Gebir*, Byron's *Childe Harold*, Thomas Moore's 1817 publication, *Lallah Rookh, An Oriental Romance*, to name three of the best-known examples; or they were romances from history, such as Scott's hugely successful *Marmion* (1808) and *The Lady of the Lake*, the latter of these appearing in the same year as *The Borough*. But what a difference is there, my countrymen. History and geography have become the here and now.

Yet as I hope I have sufficiently indicated, nobody could fairly accuse Crabbe of being a kind of statistician of life among the poor. Which isn't to say that there weren't unfair accusations along these lines – laid down by, among others, Wordsworth and Coleridge, for whom Crabbe's poems were too matter-of-fact. Yet it is precisely the facts, the phenomena of daily life, which allow Crabbe to understand his characters in a manner so startlingly new that it was left to the novelists to take up the opportunities he provided.

Meanwhile, other poets were trying various framing devices to facilitate their narrative poems. There is, for example, Robert Bloomfield. In *May Day With the Muses* (1822) Bloomfield uses the charming conceit of a benign land-owning baronet who announces he will forego the half-year land rents from all his tenants if they provide him with a May Day's entertainment of poems and tales in verse. In his Preface, Bloomfield says he is aware that Sir Ambrose's offer may seem improbable, but, he adds, tongue-in-cheek, 'a man has a right to do what he likes with his own estate', even though 'a cluster of poets is not likely to be found in one village.'

A year earlier, in his wondrous *Village Minstrel* Clare had taken the chance to narrate stories about village life among the rural poor, as, in different ways, he would do again in 1827, with *The Shepherd's Calendar*. As we have seen, Clare, who greatly admired Bloomfield, especially perhaps for his *Farmer's Boy* (1800), 'The English Theocritus,' he called him), affected to despise Crabbe for his ignorance of the rural poor, and for his part Crabbe seems to have had his doubts about Bloomfield. At all events, in sending money in 1817 to assist the newly-bankrupt poet, whose bookselling business had failed – largely because Mrs Bloomfield had given all the money she could lay her hands on to the Joanna Southcott sect – Crabbe comments, '[Bloomfield] had better rested as a shoemaker, or even a farmer's boy; for he would have been a farmer perhaps in time, and now he is an unfortunate poet.' Still, a poet may be unfortunate in material circumstances without discredit to his true work. At least Crabbe is not as dismissive as Johnson had been over James Woodhouse, 'the poetical shoemaker', who, in the great man's opinion should have stuck to his trade, 'for he may have made a good shoemaker; a poet he will never be.'

May Day With the Muses, excellent though it is, did not restore Bloomfield's fortunes. Nor did *The Shepherd's Calendar*, which included a number of 'Village stories', line Clare's pockets. As Dryden remarked, all human things are subject to decay, and so, too, are poetic styles and fashions. Clare wrote a good many tales in verse, some of which have been gathered together in recent times under the title *Cottage Tales* (1993), but by the later 1820s popular interest in such rural tales in verse was dying. So, too, I think, was a taste for the kinds of Tales Crabbe was uniquely qualified to write and which in 1819 he had brought to a new level of achievement.

The death-knell for such work was sounded in 1836, when an unknown author published *Sketches by Boz*. That changed everything.

7

Conclusion

I

With the publication of *Tales of the Hall*, Crabbe's life as a poet, at all events one in the public eye, came to an end. He wrote more verse but no other collection appeared before his death in 1832. By then, modestly famous beyond the world of Letters – Phillips' portrait of him had been exhibited in the National Academy in 1819 – he was a magistrate, he found time to visit his great admirer, Walter Scott, at Abbotsford, met both Coleridge and Wordsworth, and found himself heavily, and mistakenly, criticised in print by Hazlitt, who in an essay in the *London Magazine* for 1821 protested that 'Mr Crabbe's great fault is certainly that he is a sickly, a querulous, a fastidious poet. He sings the country, and he sings it in a pitiful tone. He chooses this subject only to take the charm out of it, and to dispel the illusion, the glory, and the dream ... If our author is a poet, why trouble himself with statistics? If he is a statistic writer, why set his ill news to harsh and grating verse?' At the end of his essay Hazlitt grudgingly admits that while Crabbe's writings 'do not add greatly to the store of entertaining and delightful fiction, yet they will remain "as a thorn in the side of poetry", perhaps for a century to come.' (CH, pp. 299-307.) But that is as far as he is prepared to go in speaking well of the poet.

Two years later, after Hazlitt had published (anonymously) his *Liber Amoris*, Crabbe wrote to his son, young George, that he thought it 'strange that any Man could write & marvellous that he could publish such History of his own Weakness, Vice and Gullibility.' But he seems to have made no direct response to Hazlitt's critical remarks. Perhaps we should not be surprised by this. He was not by nature a controversialist, and he seems to have kept away from literary circles and their accompanying and often spiteful chit-chat. If not as snug in his parsonage box as Clare imagined, he seems to have been content to steer clear of London, and, like Thomas Hardy after him, found all the material he needed for his poetry in provincial life, first in East Anglia and the midlands, and then in Somerset. 'A certain provincialism of feeling is invaluable,' Hardy wrote in a Notebook of 1880, 'it is of the essence of individuality.' Crabbe would have agreed with that, though probably wanting to add that whether provincial or metropolitan, human types – 'the worm of other class' – are replicated everywhere.

He continued to write but Murray waited for two years after the poet's death before, in 1834, he published a collection he called *Posthumous Tales*. This appeared as Vol. VIII of what was thought to be the complete *Poetical Works*, which begins with the son's charming life. Here, much is rightly made of Crabbe's love of ordinary plants – 'in botany, grasses, the most useful, but the least ornamental, were his favourites' – and it is good to learn that whenever the poet and George Jnr passed a level stretch of grass on a walk, the father would suggest they set up stumps and play a game of cricket.

As for the poems of the Posthumous collection, they are unremarkable, and prove that in having no plan to publish them Crabbe proved himself a good judge of their worth. Since then there have been at least two publications of work not included in Murray's edition. In 1960, Arthur Pollard edited *New Poems by George Crabbe*, including an inept rebuke to Byron's famous epitaph on his dog, Bosun, an exercise by his Lordship in bilious misanthropy which Crabbe attempts to counter – 'From whence, Lord B., did your Lordship find,/This horrid Picture of undone Mankind?' – but the ending of which he simply couldn't get right and as a result sensibly let the poem lie. There is also a seemingly lame attempt to write a poem in the manner of Wordsworth's 'Michael', which begins:

> In a neat Cottage hid from public View,
> Within a valley bounded by a Wood,
> Near to the Coast, but distant from a Town,
> With the kind sister of a Mother dead
> Dwelt a fair Damsel named Elizabeth.

'Upon the forest side, in Grasmere Vale,/There dwelt a shepherd, Michael was his name.' Does Crabbe intend his own poem as a parody? It is to be hoped that he did, though Pollard says nothing about this. He merely tentatively suggests 1822 as a date for the poem's composition and proposes that the following lines were 'probably suggested by the very narrow twelve-mile stretch of land bounded by the sea and the River Alde in its course from Aldborough to its outlet to the sea.' (Pollard, p.170.) These are the lines:

> … Yet there
> Were marshes all around! From that rude sea
> To that wide River! & in Time One Man
> Was ye Sole Tenant! In the narrow Farm
> Between ye Wasty bounds for many a Mile
> Bit the small hardy breed! [Of sheep]

The cod mediaevalising suggests not merely that Crabbe is writing tongue-in-cheek but that he is playing along with the then fashionable taste for such writing, one rather more effectively parodied by the novelist, Thomas Love Peacock. Crabbe doesn't seem to have mentioned Peacock in his letters or journals, but then he doesn't mention Jane Austen, either.

Other poems included in Pollard's edition are in rhyming octosyllabic quatrains or variations on this stanza form; one, in which without much conviction Crabbe indulges the vogue of 'literary' ballads, is in alternate lines of four and three stresses, and there are the inevitable narrative couplets, of which the best of a poor lot is 'David Morris'. But none of the poems begs attention. And to be fair to Pollard, he himself seems a bit defensive in claiming much for the work he has rescued, as well he might. The most he risks is a remark to the effect that the poems, since they mostly come from Crabbe's later years, 'provide a fuller picture than was hitherto available of his literary output in those years'.

Felix Pryor, the editor of *The Voluntary Insane*, a long poem of Crabbe's which was published for the first time in 1995, is far more confident about the worth of the work he has unearthed. It is, he says, 'Crabbe's masterpiece.' Why, then, did it remain unpublished for so long? Pryor explains that it was only discovered in 1989, when his father inherited a notebook which belonged 'to my great-great-great-great aunt, Sarah Hoare, who was probably Crabbe's most intimate friend in his later years.' The notebook was, in fact, Crabbe's, but the poem it contained, along with three others, could not be published because 'at the time it was written it would have been considered profoundly shocking: the more so as, distorted by nightmare, it draws on the central tragedy of Crabbe's life.'

And having prepared the ground for some startling revelation, Pryor then tells us that '*The Voluntary Insane* is a poem about a girl's madness after the death of a baby in her care. Crabbe's wife endured a similar fate. Four of her children died in infancy, causing her severe depression. After the death of a fifth, her six-year-old son William in 1796, she had a breakdown from which she never fully recovered.' Crabbe's son is then quoted. His mother, George Jnr reports, 'during the hotter months of almost every year ... was oppressed by the deepest dejection of spirits I ever witnessed in any one.' A letter Crabbe sent to a female friend is also adduced, because in it Crabbe tells his correspondent that his wife had been perfectly sane until within six months of her death, retaining the capacity for rational thought even when her mind was clouded by depression. Moreover, to close the connection between art and life, Pryor tells us that like the Maiden, who has no father but does have a rich uncle, Sarah Elmy lost her father at an early age but that a prosperous uncle took care of her upbringing. And finally, to snap the connection shut, Pryor points out that the Maiden tells her tale to a Priest and that Crabbe was himself a priest, that it is as priest-poet he narrates the Maiden's tale, and that as priest and husband Crabbe 'watched at his wife's bedside'.

Sarah Elmy's life was undoubtedly a desperately sad one, her last years made almost unbearably miserable by the loss of so many of her children. But this doesn't make *The Voluntary Insane* a masterpiece. It is a by-no-means bad poem; and, written in the form which, as Pryor notes, Crabbe tended to use for at least some of the poems where he deals in mental instability – the much earlier 'Sir Eustace Grey', for example – it further underlines his abiding concern with disorders of the psyche. But in fact the eight-line stanza, with its clasping rhymes, tends to inhibit the narrative by suggesting a literarity – a self-conscious fashioning rather like the poem in imitation of Wordsworth – which is a far remove from the realism of Crabbe's great work.

> She read of Scenes where Horror dwells,
>   Of ghostly Grief the dreadful Tale,
> Of Victims shut in Monkish Cells
>   Doomed to the Hope-Destroying Bale
> Of Prison, where the cheerful Gale
>   That plays without them never blew;

> She at such Midnight Horrors, pale
> At Midnight Reading – never grew.

Here, the verse form is perfect for the task undertaken, of mocking the self-indulgent emotions of a young woman, who, like Catherine Moreland of *Northanger Abbey* or, of course, the young woman of Crabbe's own 'The Widow's Tale', indulges a taste for sentimental or Gothic fiction in order to thrill her imagination with what were then customarily called 'pleasing horrors'.

But the very artifice of such verse, its reliance on heavily end-stopped lines and emphatic rhyme, at least in Crabbe's handling of it, looks out of place when the mood darkens.

> I now must die. My haunted Mind
> Cannot the five fold Woe sustain.
> This part I act the World to blind,
> And this dire Burden I sustain.
> The Guilt, the Trouble and the Pain
> Of Conscience! – Judge! Informer! Spy!
> And this Disease upon the brain –
> All are Life's bane! And I must die.

This would certainly lend itself to dramatic recitation. The verse is declamatory, almost melodramatic – it's easy to imagine it being spoken aloud by an actor given to histrionics – but it is quite without the varieties of address, the shifts of tone Crabbe manages in the decasyllabics of which he is a master. Tony Harrison, among others, has argued that the iambic pentameter is 'natural' to English speech rhythms. This is so, at least to the extent that you can from time to time hear people speak in perfect iambic pentameter, as I did the other day when I heard a woman at bus-stop tell a friend 'I'm going into town to buy a dress.' And while I have put the word 'natural' in inverted commas to imply a certain scepticism about the claim – there are, after all, other speech rhythms, and the woman at the bus-stop went on 'But I've promised myself I'll not go out of my way to spend more than I have to' – it would be silly to deny that iambic pentameter is certainly able to carry the modulations of the voice in a manner that is as convincing as it is expressive. What was good enough for Shakespeare …

Other metres, other line-lengths, among them some decidedly unpromising-looking ones, have been successfully recruited for speech rhythms. But it takes a ceaselessly ambitious, inquisitive and inventive kind of formalist to handle without mishap, say, the trochaic octameter, as did those virtuosi Browning (in the triplet rhyme stanzas of 'A Toccata of Galuppi's') and Hardy (in the modified terza-rima of 'Friends Beyond'). Crabbe is no such virtuoso. The decasyllabic couplet gave him all he needed. *His* inventiveness, his originality, lay, not in formal discoveries or experimentation, but in the lives he chose to write about and how, then, he wrote about them. And for this the couplet form, which as we have seen he could adapt to his own purposes, did perfectly well. You have only to think of his writing about Edward Shore, let alone Peter Grimes' broken confession of guilty consciousness, to know why *The Voluntary Insane* is a minor work. To suggest, as Pryor does, that it remained hidden because it would have been considered profoundly shocking is bunk. Who would have been shocked? Those who read Byron's *Manfred* or *The Prisoner of Chillon*, or, for that matter, *The Borough*? Hardly. And though the subject matter certainly abuts on Crabbe's own life it doesn't do so in a way that implies any betrayal of intimate secrets about his wife and her mental state. After all, Pryor quotes from the son's revelations of his mother's condition, and these were made available for public consumption two years after his father's death. Unlike the poems that make up Pollard's edition, *The Voluntary Insane* is well worth having. But it's no masterpiece.

II

By the middle of the nineteenth century, most of Crabbe's work was seen as second-rate. He could be consigned to a walk-on part in the developing history of English literature. He is not included in what is still probably the most famous anthology of English poetry, F.T. Palgrave's *The Golden Treasury of the best Songs and Lyric Poems in the English Language* (1861). And in selecting only from Songs and Lyric Poems, Palgrave may seem to be omitting a great deal else, he didn't see it that way. True poetry was, for him and others of the time, lyrical poetry. The rest was prose.

The shift in taste away from the great Augustan poets, Dryden, Pope, and, to a lesser extent, Johnson, was most damningly signalled by Matthew Arnold's claim that they were classics of an age of prose rather than of poetry. This is the context in which to consider the long, and for the most part dismissive, essay on Crabbe by W.C. Roscoe that appeared in 1859 in *The National Review*. Roscoe repeats many of the criticisms that Crabbe had to endure during his lifetime. 'His remarks are all detached,' Roscoe claims. 'He collected the materials for his poetry in just the same way as he collected his facts in science.' Not only that. 'His writings cannot be said to be distinguished either by wit or humour.' (CH, p. 408.) Well, as Empson said of David Holbrook's claim that Dylan Thomas had no sense of rhythm, 'I'm afraid I can't help him there.'

Other critics were more sympathetic, especially perhaps the one who in 1869 in *St James's Magazine* rightly said that 'Crabbe was meant and made for what he did: to be the poet of the poorer, darker, rougher side of humanity, and not only to draw the picture, but to say all that he felt and could to soothe and to relieve the burden, to expose the folly, to lay bare the fraud; and he did it well.' (CH, pp. 422-3). This rather over-emphasises Crabbe the moraliser, Crabbe the priest, but the praise for Crabbe of the 'uncomfortable mind', to use Forster's memorable phrase, Crabbe the poet of the dark side of humanity is well taken, though as we have seen, he could also write wonderfully well about other matters. To say this is to say that he is a much more various poet than is commonly allowed. Yes, he is 'Nature's sternest painter, and her best', but as Jane Austen and Dickens in particular understood, he is also and perhaps supremely, a poet who is a great novelist in verse.

Perhaps, though, it is better to repeat what I have stressed throughout this account of his work: Crabbe's especial virtues are ones that anticipate much that will go to the making of the great realist fictions of the nineteenth century, and that, for all the criticisms of his concern with 'mere matters of fact', his achievement never betrays the medium of verse. He is, in other words, a great poet, one whose natural métier is the verse tale and the exploration of other lives, other circumstances. As such, he is up there with Chaucer and Browning.

And I don't think you can go higher than that.

Bibliography

a) Crabbe's Works

In quoting from Crabbe's poetry I have wherever possible used the first editions of his Poems, which I have on my shelves, supplemented by the 1807 edition of *Poems* and the Penguin *George Crabbe: Selected Poems*, edited by Gavin Edwards, 1991. I have also used my own Selection, made for Longman in 1967, frequently re-printed until the late 1980s, and copies of which can still be found, plus Arthur Pollard's edition of *New Poems*, 1960. (Poems which came to light in the years following Murray's publication of *Posthumous Tales*.) Norma Dalrymple-Champneys and Pollard's edition of *The Complete Poetical Works* appeared in 1988, but has, of course, been made more complete by Felix Pryor's edition of *The Voluntary Insane*, 1995.

For the Prose, I have used Thomas C. Faulkner's edition of *Selected Letters and Journals*, 1985.

b) Biography

Neil Powell's full biography, published in 2004 (re-printed 2014) is excellent, though the *Life* by Crabbe's son, which first appeared in 1834, and has been since reprinted in the twentieth century by the Cresset Press, remains a delightful account of a man I wish I had been able to meet.

c) Criticism

Arthur Pollard's *George Crabbe: The Critical Heritage*, 1972, is essential, and of modern studies, two can be recommended, Peter New's *George Crabbe's Poetry*, 1976, and Gavin Edwards'

George Crabbe's Poetry on Border Land, 1990. And E.M. Forster's essay on Crabbe in *Two Cheers for Democracy*, 1951, is well worth reading.

Note

Benjamin Britten's opera, *Peter Grimes*, libretto by Montagu Slater, is one of the composer's best-known works. As I have indicated in my discussion of *The Borough* I am less sure of its worth than most. The incidental music is wonderful, some of the arias splendid, but overall it seems to me muddled. Grimes is presented as an outcast, a bully, and a murderer, but he is somehow still meant to be sympathetic. There is, I suspect, not merely a gay sub-text to this but, bearing in mind Slater's communist sympathies, a desire to suggest that Grimes is an outsider because he can't fit into the society of his native place, one characterised by petty-minded, bourgeois morality. Crabbe doesn't shirk the petty-mindedness of at least some members of that society, of those who, on 'hearing cries,/Said calmly "Grimes is at his exercise."' But that doesn't excuse Grimes. If anything, it boosts his sense of invulnerability. Crabbe's view is resolutely un-sentimental, darker and truer to unregenerate human nature, I would say, than his twentieth-century interpreters. And without wishing to be unduly provocative, I will add that in the latter half of the 1940s, Britten, the pacifist, and Slater, the apologist for Stalin's Russia, might not have wanted to confront the uncomfortable truths of murderous behaviour for which the just-finished war had provided overwhelming evidence.

SELECTED LITERARY TITLES
from GREENWICH EXCHANGE

W.H. DAVIES
Man and Poet: A Reassessment

Michael Cullup

978-1-906075-88-0 (pbk)
146pp

Even though he was once one of Britain's most popular writers, the reputation of the poet and memoirist W.H. Davies has, in recent decades, gone into decline.

Davies's colourful early life as a hobo and a tramp – captured by his most famous work *The Autobiography of a Super Tramp* – and his apparently 'innocent' poems about nature, tales about the seamier sides of life, his experiences on the road and verse portraits of those characters he met there – has led to the Welsh poet being placed under the cosy heading 'Georgian'.

It has been a tag which does serious disservice to the tone, nature and ambition of Davies's lyrics.

As poet and critic Michael Cullup shows in this brief but insightful exploration of the entirety of Davies's output – the memoirs, the short stories as well as the poems – there was a more complex personality than the one suggested by his public persona. True, he was a figure at home with the Georgian literary world – Edward Thomas and Hilaire Belloc were close friends – yet he was also capable of impressing more avant-garde talents like Ezra Pound and Jacob Epstein.

In this bracing reappraisal Cullup judiciously undermines preconceived notions of Davies the writer to reveal a poetic imagination richer, more insightful, more thoughtful than that for which he is generally given credit.

RAYMOND CHANDLER

Anthony Fowles

978-1-906075-87-3 (pbk)
206pp

The position of Raymond Chandler in the pantheon of American letters has long been subject to much debate.

Naturally imbued with a literary sensibility Chandler helped to revolutionise the crime genre, bringing to it a colourful, hardedged vernacular allied to a modern social commentary.

Through the figure of private eye Philip Marlowe, Chandler created a contemporary knight errant whose not so picturesque adventures trudging the mean streets of Los Angeles helped to vividly define the moral dilemmas of a dark, uncertain post-war world.

And yet ... can *The Big Sleep, Farewell, My Lovely* and *The Lady in the Lake* be considered 'literature'?

Author Anthony Fowles – who freely admits to writing half-a-dozen 'sub-Chandlerian' thrillers – brings to the discussion both the detached eye of the professional critic and the sympathetic understanding of the practitioner.

It is a background which allows Fowles to make a balanced, finely-nuanced contribution to the ongoing Chandler debate, refusing to relegate the noir master to the wilderness of 'genre writer' but equally avoiding outlandish claims of literary pre-eminence.

In circumventing the pitfalls and simplicities of 'either/or', Fowles places Chandler's achievements in a fully-realised context, enabling the reader to appreciate more deeply the peculiar strengths and limitations of the prose lyricist of the American mid-century.

SWEETLY SINGS DELANEY

A Study of Shelagh Delaney's Work, 1958-68

John Harding

978-1-906075-83-5 (pbk)
204pp

Shelagh Delaney rose to fame following the instant success in 1958 of her first play *A Taste of Honey*. Lauded as Britain's answer to the controversial French novelist Françoise Sagan, Delaney's work scandalised her home city of Salford but established her as one of the country's most original and exhilarating young playwrights during a period in theatre history when women writers were rare and acceptance hard to achieve.

Delaney has served as an inspiration to countless young artists down the succeeding years. Rock star Morrissey wrote, 'She has always been a part of my life as a perfect example of how to get up and get out and do it.' Novelist Jeanette Winterson claimed, 'She was like a lighthouse – pointing the way and warning about the rocks underneath.'

Sweetly Sings Delaney is the story of her first exciting decade as a writer when she not only produced challenging and dramatic work in prose and on stage but also collaborated with some of the most innovative film and documentary-makers of the decade such as Ken Russell, Tony Richardson, Lindsay Anderson, not to mention actor and fellow Salfordian Albert Finney during his first and only foray as a film director.

JOHN KEATS
Against All Doubtings

Andrew Keanie

978-1-906075-75-0 (pbk)
110pp

Having identified him as a sort of semi-educated little cockney chancer, Keats's contemporary reviewers savaged him in the pages of Britain's most influential magazines. High ambition, unaccompanied by high birth, and radical affiliations and liberal inclinations, made him an object of contempt to those of, or aping the opinions of, the literary Establishment. In the short term, he never stood a chance.

Long after his death, his reputation was eventually brightened by much more enthusiastic – if, as some have since argued, misguided – appreciations for his beautiful and powerful otherworldliness.

Later still, in reaction to Keats-lovers' gushing admiration, a much more worldly Keats has been written up – including some bracing insights that seem to owe something to his first reviewers. As Martin Seymour-Smith has said, 'Many privately regard [Keats] with a condescension that is more smug than they would like to admit.'

This largely text-focused study promotes the best energies of a more Romantic view of a key Romantic figure. Keats was inspired and ill. By the time of his death, his genius and tuberculosis had pressurised him into poetry. The best he had to offer – including searching and scintillating confidences concerning how to live one's life in this world of suffering, 'the Vale of Soul-making' – are more accessible to the reader with a taste for poetry than they are to the consumer of ideologically appropriate journalism or ostentatiously unemotional academic analyses.

SECOND WORLD WAR POETRY IN ENGLISH

John Lucas

978-1-906075-78-1 (pbk)
236pp

John Lucas's book sets out to challenge the widely-held assumption that the poetry of the Second World War is, at best, a poor relation to that produced by its predecessor. He argues that the best poetry that came out of the 1939-45 war, while very different from the work of Owen, Rosenberg, Gurney, and their contemporaries, is in no sense inferior. It also has different matters to consider. War in the air, war at sea, war beyond Europe, the politics of Empire, democratic accountability – these are no subjects to be found in the poetry of the Great War. Nor is sex. Nor did American poets have much to say about that war, whereas the Americans Randall Jarrell, Anthony Hecht and Louis Simpson, are among the greatest English-speaking poets of World War Two. Both Hecht and Simpson write about the Holocaust and its aftermath, as do the English poets, Lotte Kramer and Gerda Mayer. For these reasons among others, English-speaking poetry of the Second World War deserves to be valued as work of unique importance.

A.E. HOUSMAN

Spoken and Unspoken Love

Henry Maas

978-1-906075-71-2 (pbk)
978-1-906075-73-6 (hbk)
61pp

A Shropshire Lad by A.E. Housman is one of the best-loved books of poems in English, but even now its author remains a shadowy figure. He maintained an iron reserve about himself – and with good reason. His emotional life was dominated by an unhappy and unrequited love for an Oxford friend. His passion went into his writing, but he could barely hint at its cause. *Spoken and Unspoken Love* discusses all Housman's poetry, especially the effect of an existence deprived of love, as seen in the posthumous work, where the story becomes clear in personal and deeply moving poems.

ERNEST DOWSON

Poetry and Love in the 1890s

Henry Maas

978-1-906075-51-4 (pbk)
978-1-906075-73-6 (hbk)
48pp

Ernest Dowson is the archetypal poet of the 1890s. His best work comes entirely from the decade, and he died at the end of it.

Steeped in the Latin poets of antiquity and French 19th-century poetry, he developed an individual style which pared down the exuberance of Poe and Swinburne to a classical simplicity marked by meticulous attention to sound and initiating the move to more informal verse, which made his work attractive to the generation of D.H. Lawrence, Pound and Eliot.

His life was archetypal too. Born to respectable wealth and comfort, he was dragged down by family misfortune. His father's business failure and early death, his mother's suicide and his own advancing tuberculosis began the decline. It was hastened by drink and an impossible love for a young girl who never began to understand him.

In the end Dowson, the poet admired by Yeats, Wilde and a host of contemporaries, was reduced to living little better than a tramp in Paris, to die at thirty-two almost a pauper and alcoholic in a London workman's cottage, leaving posterity some of the finest love poetry in English.

BETWEEN TWO WORLDS

A Survey of Writing in Britain, 1900-1914

Hugh Underhill

978-1-906075-55-2 (pbk)
188pp

In 1924 Philip Gibbs, one of the first 'war correspondents' in the modern sense, wrote in his book *Ten Years After: A Reminder*, 'One has to think back to another world in order to see again that year 1914 before the drums of war began to beat. It is a different world now ... ' A certain popular view has persisted of the Edwardian and pre-war Georgian period as a kind of swan-song to a past elegance and grace, and one of pleasure and freedom from anxiety.

The reality, along with, for many, the leisurely pace and settled way of life, was not only one of great intellectual and artistic excitement, but also of unrest, change and controversy. The first section of this survey, 'Britain 1900-1914: Hope, ferment and the abyss', looks at the political, cultural and economic elements of that ferment and the strains evident in British society: the reaction against Victorian attitudes, the pressure for social reform, the campaigns for women's suffrage and Irish Home Rule, the stirrings of Modernism and the move towards social realism in literature and the arts.

Underhill vividly demonstrates how these forces fed into the writing of the period. In the second section of the book, the work of the major authors of the period, Bennett, Wells, Conrad, Forster, Lawrence, Joyce, James, Shaw, Synge, Yeats, Hardy and Edward Thomas, is critically surveyed.

This is followed, in the final section, by a resumé of the work and varying significance of other authors against which those major figures need to be seen.

OTHER TITLES OF INTEREST

STORY
The Heart of the Matter
Maggie Butt (editor)
978-1-871551-93-8 (pbk)   184pp

MATTHEW ARNOLD AND 'THYRSIS'
Patrick Carill Connolly
978-1-871551-61-7 (pbk)   204pp

MILTON'S *PARADISE LOST*
Peter Davies
978-1-906075-47-7 (pbk)   108pp

LIAR! LIAR!
Jack Kerouac – Novelist
R.J. Ellis
978-1-871551-53-2 (pbk)   294pp

JOHN DRYDEN
Anthony Fowles
978-1-871551-58-7 (pbk)   292pp

THE AUTHOR, THE BOOK & THE READER
Robert Giddings
987-1-871551-01-3 (pbk)   240pp

POETRY MASTERCLASS
John Greening
978-1-906075-58-3   142pp

DREAMING OF BABYLON

The Life and Times of Ralph Hodgson

John Harding

978-1-906075-00-2 (pbk)   238pp

WORDSWORTH AND COLERIDGE

Views from the Meticulous to the Sublime

Andrew Keanie

978-1-871551-87-7 (pbk)   206pp

POETRY IN EXILE

A Study of the Poetry of Auden, Brodsky & Szirtes

Michael Murphy

978-1-871551-76-1 (pbk)   270pp

ALEISTER CROWLEY AND THE CULT OF PAN

Paul Newman

978-1-871551-66-2 (pbk)   224pp

IN PURSUIT OF LEWIS CARROLL

Raphael Shaberman

978-1-871551-13-6 (pbk)   146pp

To find out more about these and other titles visit
www.greenex.co.uk